UNCORKED

The Novice's Guide to Wine

UNCORKED

The Novice's Guide to Wine

Paul Kreider

TURNER
PUBLISHING COMPANY

Turner Publishing Company

445 Park Avenue, 9th Floor
New York, NY 10022
Phone: (646)291-8961   Fax: (646)291-8962

200 4th Avenue North, Suite 950
Nashville, TN 37219
Phone: (615)255-2665   Fax: (615)255-5081

Uncorked: The Novice's Guide to Wine

www.turnerpublishing.com

Cover design by Mike Penticost

Library of Congress Cataloging-in-Publication Data

Kreider, Paul, 1945-
Uncorked : the novice's guide to wine / Paul Kreider.
   p. cm.
ISBN 978-1-59652-814-7
1. Wine and wine making. 2. Drinking customs. I. Title.
TP548.K7355 2011
641.2'2--dc22

                                2010050855

Printed in the United States of America

12 13 14 15 16 17 18 — 0 9 8 7 6 5 4 3 2

To my brother and sisters, Bruce, Lynn, Jeanne, Patti, and Phyllis, and my winemaking apprentice Kerry Kirkham, who have all faithfully—and each in their own way—supported me and the winery in the years of our development.

Wine is constant proof that God loves us and loves to see us happy.
—Benjamin Franklin

Contents

Introduction

Wine has graced our tables and delighted man for ages.

Evidence of the first grape wine cultivation was discovered in the Caucasus Mountains in a place bordered by the Caspian, Mediterranean, and Black seas. This area encompasses the Tigris and Euphrates Valley, the center of man's first successful efforts in agriculture during the shift from a nomadic to an agrarian society. This early cultivation dates to around 5000 or 6000 B.C., about 7,000 to 8,000 years ago.

From those beginnings, wine has had ample opportunity to become a complex and intimidating subject despite the fact that fundamentally, it is simply fermented grape juice.

In the same way that other disciplines (e.g., computer technology) manifest disciples who endeavor to protect their knowledge and speak in code or a language that others do not readily understand, wine enthusiasts use specialized words to convey their enjoyment and understanding of wine, their passion.

When reading this book, you will educate yourself and thus enable yourself to enjoy more of what wine has to offer in its magnificent complexity. You'll be able to walk into wineries, wineshops, and wine bars and be at ease because you will have gained valuable rudimentary wine knowledge. This knowledge will also assist you in making choices that suit your palate, thus saving you money in the long run. You'll finally know what you're looking for in wine and be able to express that clearly.

This book is real and unpretentious, the straight story on wine. You will not need to be an oenologist (scientist of winemaking), nor will you need to be a viticulturist (scientist of wine grape growing), a chemist, or any other specialist in order to enjoy and learn from this little book.

When people ask me, "Where did you learn about wine?" my answer is usually, "The same place you learned to cook." Most of us learn to cook in little steps over time by experimenting, reading, asking questions, and pursuing our own intellectual curiosity. Let this book be one of those steps in your wine education. When you are comfortable with what you know, swim deeper. You will never reach the bottom of the knowledge pool.

This book will investigate many aspects of wine. During this discussion, some key words will appear in bold, emphasizing important terms to remember when wine is discussed. Their definitions should be self-evident from the paragraphs in which they are used, but for easy reference, these words are listed at the back of the book with the page reference to where they are described.

I know that you will remember most of them—this isn't rocket science—but should you hear an unfamiliar term at a tasting or from a friend, make a mental—or even better, a written—note for future reference.

In this book, I refer to several Web sites. In case you begin thinking otherwise, these URLs I am sharing have no commercial connection to me; rather, the businesses have had the fortune to be ones whose products or information I have used and think favorably of.

A simple French lesson

The world of wine is saturated with French words for one good reason: France is the motherland of wine. Oh, yes, other countries have been giving her a run for her money in the past few decades, but the French have been consistently making extraordinary, distinctive wines for well over 600 years, so a few decades are relatively unimportant. It is difficult to encounter any wine enthusiast and not hear at least a few words of French origin.

In order to avoid misunderstanding, increase your scope, and clue you in to a basic understanding of the pronunciation of the language, I offer you this simple rule: with only one exception I can think of, final single consonants are not pronounced in French. This means, as you may have already discovered, that the word *merlot* is pronounced "mer-lo" and not "mer-lot." *Caberet* is "cab-er-ay" and the same goes for cabernet, "cab-er-nay." Pinot is "peeno," not "pee-not," and noir is "nwah," not "no-wire."

Here's a good one: *terroir,* a French term for the uniqueness of geography, the weather, and the soil in which a wine's grapes are grown. It is pronounced "tare-wa," not, as I have heard, "terror." Likewise, *fermez* is "fer-mey," *gris* is "gree," and *Chevrolet* is, well, you know how it is pronounced.

The only exception to this pronunciation rule that a couple of my French-speaking patrons and I can think of is *cheval,* the word for horse, which is pronounced, "sha-val." (However, I am certain I will be hearing about other exceptions from some of my readers.)

With your newfound knowledge, you will be pleased to understand that the word noir—black—and *noix*—nuts—are pronounced the same . . . or almost the same. The French add a nasal intonation at the end of *noir,* sort of echoing up their nasal cavity to distinguish these final consonants. It takes practice and a certain Gallic swashbuckling, but you'll get the hang of it and will soon be talking with nasal intonations yourself. And that might be interesting in Atlanta, Mobile, or Nashville.

This valuable lesson alone is well worth the price of this book, as it will open the language door of wine to you in a way that is easy to understand so that you will be able to interface more easily with the wine community.

Uncorked

1
Drinking and tasting

1

Drinking and tasting

Drinking wine is different from tasting wine. The words "wine tasting" conjure up an image of people holding crystal wineglasses while peering, sniffing, sipping, and slurping the wine. The phrase "wine drinking" conjures up the image of people sitting around a food-laden table, quaffing glasses of wine while they eat and talk.

The difference between those two scenarios is that the wine tasters are focusing attention on the characteristics of their wine and enjoying it in all its complexity, while the drinkers are simply enjoying it. There is nothing inappropriate about quaffing wine with food. In fact, that is why we winemakers make it. It is a beverage that uniquely enhances food, conversation, and conviviality.

Tasting wine is simply drinking wine at a different level, usually in less volume. It is a different kind of enjoyment based on discovering the nuances in a glass and a taste of wine. An analogy might be the difference between speed-reading a Robert Frost poem and being attentive to its poetic details, alliteration, rhyme, meter, symbols, and imagery. Once you are versed in these details, you will never be able to read or hear that poem in the same way again. And the same is true of wine. The more you discover about it, the greater your appreciation of it.

And that's what we are discovering in this book: wine appreciation. To appreciate wine is to differentiate one from another, discovering specific characteristics and defining your senses enough to make a personal, subjective decision that you like one better, and why. I did not write "that the wine you like is better" because the wine in your glass may be better to you, but the person next to you probably has different likes and dislikes and tastes differently than you because he or she has a different palate. So let's not start a brawl at the tasting bar because you think your opinion is the only one that matters. However, I would agree that your opinion is the only one that matters when it comes to you purchasing a bottle. That is what wine tasting is all about: understanding why you are making a decision and being able to articulate it.

As we navigate together through this book, I will come back to the premise that the more you know about wine, the more you will enjoy it. Like understanding a poem, a painting, or the history of Rome before visiting, understanding the information hidden in wine will enhance your enjoyment of it.

2

Don't trust your first sip

2

Don't trust your first sip

Now that you know the preliminary step of wine tasting—to focus all your senses on the characteristics of what is in your glass—I am going to throw you a curve: never trust your first taste of a wine.

Your taste will be strongly influenced by what you last had in your mouth. If that was toothpaste, it doesn't take much imagination to realize how your palate will react to an acidic beverage. However, there are other common influences that will throw your palate out of kilter. At the top of this list are coffee, mints, and chocolate. It is interesting that dark chocolate actually enhances the flavors of some wines, but those are usually not the wines with which you would start your tasting flight.

How do you clear your palate before approaching your flight deck? The simplest approach is to chew on some bread, an unseasoned cracker, or a breadstick. Then rinse your mouth with water and you are ready for takeoff. Still, the first taste of wine is a transitional one for your palate; wait for your second taste from the same glass before making taste judgments—you can apply all your other senses without concern.

When you encounter tasters who are mostly concerned with tasting red wines, you may find them warming up their palates with a small amount of white wine, not a bad practice if your interest is in heavier tannic reds.

Aside from the caution about trusting your first taste of a wine, there is another wine tasting issue that has to do with *order*. In a typical wine lineup, the wines should be arranged in order from lightest to heaviest, starting with the lighter-flavored whites such as sauvignon blanc and pinot grigio (a.k.a. pinot gris) and increasing to the heaviest reds, cabernet sauvignon, malbec, and some zinfandels.

The reason this order should be followed is so your palate can adjust from a lighter wine to a heavier wine, resulting in a more accurate and enjoyable taste. If you go too far backwards, from a cabernet sauvignon to a chardonnay, for example, you will find the chardonnay most unpleasant after the big red, no matter what you thought of it in the first tasting.

If you are a passionate chef—and it is evident that a huge percentage of people who are passionate about food are also passionate about wine—this palate adjustment is not news to you. You would probably not serve a spicy pickled red cabbage dish with a fragrant and delicate veal filet. The extreme differences between those two flavors to your palate would make for a jarring combination, enhancing neither.

3

Why red is red and white isn't

3

Why red is red and white isn't

Do you remember asking as a child, "Daddy, does chocolate milk come from brown cows?" Unless your dad had a particularly strange sense of humor, he gently set you straight. So when people ask me (quite more often than you'd guess) whether white wine comes from white grapes and red wine from red ones, I have to secretly smile my brown cow smile and answer the question sincerely.

Here is the straight information from winemaker

to you: "sometimes" is used to respond to this question because the winemaker, a sort of chef d'grapes, has a large number of process options available in his kitchen and winery, and winemakers all follow a slightly different recipe or process that results in subtly different wines, even if made from the same batch of grapes.

The juice of all grapes is neither red nor white; it is translucent and without much color. There is one exception, Alicante Bouchet, an obscure varietal whose juice is deep red from the start.

When white grapes are crushed—that is, removed from their stems and their skins broken to release their juice—they are pressed either immediately or sometimes after a day or so of grape–skin contact. The resulting pressed juice, having been separated from the skins, is fermented into wine in a barrel or tank. When it is finished fermenting, it is considered white wine, or more accurately, a shade of light straw or very faint green.

On the other hand, red grapes are crushed and the juice is left with the skins to ferment for a week or sometimes much longer. It is during this juice–skin contact that the red color is extracted from the skins and into the liquid, becoming red wine. When fermentation is complete, the wine is pressed from the skins, and the liquid is allowed to settle in a barrel or tank.

Now here's what's neat: some varieties of red grapes are crushed with their juice immediately removed from the skins and fermented separately. The result is a wine that is "white," or close to it, depending on the grapes. Champagne is sometimes made partially from pinot noir, a red grape, as well as a few other varietals that are red skinned and made into wine in this manner.

At one point, this process was the true source of what we call "blush wines" because the juice cannot be separated from some varietals of ripe, red grapeskins fast enough to avoid some pink color transfer. From this, a very popular new wine category was born, the blush wines, of which "white" zinfandel was by far the favorite. So great was its influence that even today, people, mostly from the middle part of the country, still come into my tasting room and express surprise that zinfandel is red.

Blush wines have almost always had residual sweetness and have been embraced by the sugar-loving young adults who've had their palates skewed to favor sweetness by consuming soft drinks for most of their lives. As these adults' palates developed, the blushes became ideal for their first wine experience. But the palate soon tires of sweet, and so one ventures to something different.

4

Wines your (grand) parents drank

4

Wines your (grand)parents drank

I'm old enough to remember parents of friends saying before dinner, "Let's have a glass of burgundy," and then pouring glasses full from a large jug.

In their efforts to market wine when the wine experience was in its adolescence stage in America, domestic wineries decided to use wine names that were familiar to the largely European ethnic customers who drank wine as a matter of course. So they applied labels with famous wine names to their jugs.

Although American wines named burgundy, chablis, champagne, chianti, and sauterne bore no resemblance whatsoever to the noble wines of those famous regions, apparently the words were familiar enough to make the wine-drinking population buy the jugs. Wine marketing being what it is, the story didn't end there.

Champagne is the brand of wine made, by French law, only in Champagne, France. The Champagne producers (note the capital "C") fired the first salvo with ads reminding people that champagne could only come from the French district of the same name, and that all other wine with bubbles was called "sparkling wine." California responded with a sparkling product called "California champagne" that satisfied the letter of the law issue, if not the intent of the law.

For decades, wines were marketed in the U.S. with names like hearty burgundy, petit chablis, and port. As a rule, these wines, at least the ones on the West Coast, were made from inexpensive Central Valley grapes. Although lacking the entire flavor profile, they filled the need for inexpensive wine to be consumed without any pretension. As a result, the European "owners" of those place-names were frustrated because they had no authority to regulate the wines made and sold in the U.S.

Finally, in March 2006, the U.S. government reached an agreement with the European Community (the EC) that those place-names would not be used on U.S. wines (www.wineinstitute.org/resources/exports/article61). The old, previously approved labels were grandfathered into the agreement, allowing those labels to be used by the wineries that held them, as long as the labels were not changed by new ownership or design. That's why you can still go to the supermarket and purchase a four-liter jug labeled "burgundy." (We will look at the informative subject of labels more closely in the next chapter in this book.)

In the larger scheme of things, using others' names on American wines was actually beneficial to all wine-producing countries. The inexpensive jugs encouraged people to start drinking wine with meals, which led to their discovery of nicer wines and then to European wines with those old familiar names. Currently, the U.S. is a huge producer of its own premium wines but is also an extremely important market for those true champagnes, burgundies, chablis, chiantis, sauternes, and ports.

5

Wine labels

5
Wine labels

When you walk into your local wineshop, supermarket, or wherever your state allows you to buy wine, it seems you are greeted by an avalanche of colorful labels, catchy names, and bright colors. It may seem overwhelming, but in this chapter you are going to learn that each of those labels contains valuable information that will help you make a purchasing decision based on what you are looking for rather than a decision based on a graphic artist's attempt to grab your attention.

Here's a fact that may blow your mind: every single label you see on that shelf—indeed, every label on wine sold in the U.S.—has been scrutinized and approved by the U.S. government. The agency responsible, operating under the Department of Treasury, is the Tobacco and Alcohol Tax and Trade Bureau, TTB for short. This replaced the BATF (Bureau of Alcohol, Tobacco and Firearms), which governed those three regulated products. The TTB checks for specific information printed in a specific minimum-size font on each label. The winery certifies that the information is correct and is subject to audit for verification. Lest you think this is an empty threat, let me tell you that my tiny winery has been audited three times for label verification. Not a treat.

Here are the specific data the agency looks for on a wine label submitted for a Certificate of Label Approval **(COLA)**, along with information you can count on as you further your wine education.

*The **varietal** of grapes used to make the wine.* A varietal is a standard variety of grape. If the label says chardonnay, then at least 75 percent of the grapes in the wine must be the varietal chardonnay. Surprised at the 75 percent? When I started making wine, the percentage requirement was only 51, which meant that 49 percent of your "chardonnay" could legally be a less desirable and way less expensive varietal such as Thompson Seedless or French Colombard filler grapes. The change to 75 percent represented a quality of product movement to more elegant wines. It is not uncommon to find a blended wine without any varietal designation at all. This is because none of the components of that wine make up 75 percent of the mix. However, these blended wines are not necessarily inferior wines.

The place from where the grapes originated. This is called the **appellation,** from the French word of the same name (no surprise there). It indicates the designated area in which the grapes were grown. If your wine bottle says "Sonoma Valley" before the varietal of grape, as in "Sonoma Valley Chardonnay," then 85 percent of the grapes must be from the Sonoma Valley. Generally speaking, the tighter the location, the more identifiable the characteristics of the wine. For example, the Russian River Valley is a small appellation within the larger appellation of Sonoma County, and a winery would naturally use that smaller name in its nomenclature if 85 percent or more of the grapes came from there. The valley, therefore, identifies the source of the grapes more closely. If your wine says "California Chardonnay," the grapes could have come from anywhere in the state—again, not necessarily a bad thing. An even more exact appellation would be the specific vineyard the grapes were harvested from. This *vineyard designation* is a further statement of quality, as 95 percent of the grapes must be from that specific vineyard.

The year that the grapes were harvested, also known as the **vintage.** This is an identifier of quality as well and gives the consumer the opportunity to remark not just on a winery and varietal of wine, but also on the year of harvest, as in, "That '97 Parsons Vineyard zinfandel was incredible; got any more for sale?" The grapes in that bottle must be 100 percent from that vintage. If more than one year's are used, the wine is identified as *non-vintage,* or *NV* for short. These are also not to be looked down upon, necessarily.

The alcohol content. All wineries pay a per-gallon

excise tax on their wines, with the rate depending on their size (smaller ones get a break) and on the alcohol content of the wine. Up to 14 percent alcohol is taxed at a lower rate, currently $1.17 per gallon, while 14 percent and over is taxed at $1.67 per gallon. From the consumer's standpoint, this information indicates several things, not the least important of which is how many glasses you may be able to consume with dinner and still be able to legally drive home in your county or state. You should know that the percentage number has a leeway of 1.5 percent either direction from what is printed on the label, as long as the 14 percent number is not exceeded, at which point the tax class changes.

There is a required minimum font size for alcohol information to be printed on the label—three millimeters—but it is often darn hard to find, let alone read. However, without it there, the TTB will not issue the certificate of approval. In place of the alcohol percentage, you may find the words "table wine," a broad category for wines below 14 percent alcohol.

What winery bottled the wine and where that was done. Don't confuse this information with the brand of the wine. "Golden Glen Cellars," usually in large, fancy print on the front of the bottle, may not actually exist other than as a brand name whose wines are made and bottled all over the state. Look for the words "produced and bottled by" or some variation of that phrase and for a city and state. "Produced and bottled by" designates that that wine was made by that bonded winery and was bottled at that winery location. Why is this important? If you want consistency in your wines, you can assume that if the winery itself made and controlled all the production and bottling from year to year, the product you got five years ago should be fairly close to the wine you buy today. If the "produced and bottled by" line says anything else—"cellared by," "blended by," "perfected by," or "made and bottled by"—then the winery did not make all of that wine on its premises. It is possible that they ran out of fermentation space and leased some space in the bonded winery up the road and could therefore not use the "produced" designation. That's possible, but it is far more likely that the winery bought that wine as bulk wine in a tank truck and bottled it at their winery. This is not necessarily a bad thing for the consumer. Many of the very inexpensive and some not-so-inexpensive bottles on the supermarket shelves have this designation. They are inexpensive mostly because the winery did not make the investment in grapes, labor, and fermentation to bottle and sell the wine. Some of these wines are pleasant to drink, but usually the motivation to market them is cash flow.

The words "contains sulfites" (which we will examine closely elsewhere).

The government warning, a strictly formatted statement by the government which warns you not to drink alcohol if you are pregnant, nor to drive a vehicle or operate machinery after consuming the wine (there is at least some evidence that these warnings are merited), and finally, that consumption "may cause health problems." This information is required on every bottle of wine sold in the U.S., despite some documented evidence to the contrary. It's a regulated industry, and the government, whether motivated or directed by a Quaker surgeon general or a born-again prohibitionist, has the power to dictate to the wine industry certain requirements.

I often tell people I really became interested in wine when I was eighteen after returning from a trip to Europe, where I discovered that wine (and beer) was treated as a food rather than a crime as it often is in the U.S. I was impressed that parents included their children in family toasts, dinners, and celebrations where wine and beer was consumed. In fairness, I did not see children knocking back shots of schnapps. It seemed like having a little wine or beer with the folks at dinner was a healthy thing, as opposed to forbidding it to young adults until they reach twenty-one, at which point many go crazy with their new experience and end up driving cars into brick walls. Because it was available with meals and parents were present, it wasn't such a big thing. I liked that attitude and raised my children, successfully and without alcohol incident, with that ideology.

Chapter 6

How can wine, a liquid, be dry?

6

How can wine, a liquid, be dry?

This is a case of one of those specialized words that wine people use to communicate among themselves about wine. These specialized words can be confusing and intimidating because they are words you know in only one context—you know that dry means not wet—but these words have a different meaning when applied to wine.

Here is the straight info: to a winemaker, **dry** is the opposite of "sweet" and occurs when the grapes ferment completely, meaning there is no sugar left in their juice. The resulting wine is "dry."

Wine novices sometimes confuse the term "dry" with the sensation some wines bring to their palate in which the wine seems to dry out their mouths like cotton. This sensation, mostly along the sides and back of the tongue, is caused by **tannin**. **Tannic acid** comes from the skins, seeds, and stems of the grape as well as from the oak barrels in which the juice may have been aged. As we have seen, white wine is fermented off the skins as juice, so white wines have little tannin and should not show this characteristic unless they have been oak-barrel aged, in which case they would only mildly produce tannin. Wines with too much tannin are termed **tannic** and benefit from proper bottle aging to "smooth out the tannins."

Winemakers sometimes work hard to put tannin into their wines because tannin gives the wine **structure,** or several layers of complementary flavors. As an acid, it is also a preservative. Like most things in life, though, too much of a good thing isn't always so good, so we try to modify the winemaking so the wine is in **balance,** meaning that no one attribute of the wine stands out so much that it overpowers the others.

7

The color is not just red and white

7

The color is not just red and white

Wouldn't you know it? All these years you have been asking for a "glass of red" or a "glass of white" and pretty much getting what you want, and now I come along to tell you there is much, much more involved in the color of the wine you are drinking.

First, let's establish that red wine is not red, but some shade of garnet, ruby, or burgundy (how's that for redundancy?). Red is the color of some of the stripes in our nation's flag. That's not the color of wine, any more than the color of the flag's other stripes is the color of white wine. "White" wine tends to be a faint shade of yellow, straw, or even green.

In learning about wine, we need to pay attention to the real color of what's in our glass. It really helps to do this observing against a white background, something as simple as flipping a piece of paper over to its blank side. Hold the glass at an angle against the paper and look at it where the edge of the wine meets the glass, known as its **meniscus.** The wine's true colors will be revealed to you. And in revealing themselves, this revelation of color gives you some additional information.

If it is a red varietal, that is, the type or kind of red grape, the color will be a shade of deep plum on the white background. If that plum color goes evenly out to the edge, it is of sufficient bottle age to be enjoyed now; it's neither too young nor too old.

If perhaps you notice a brown tint at the edge of the wine, the wine reveals itself to be somewhat older if it has been stored properly; you can expect a more mellow red wine. This is also to be enjoyed, because the brown (as long as it isn't too brown) represents a matured, slightly **oxidized** aged wine.

If it has a violet tint, the edge is telling you that the wine is an infant, very young and fruity with almost no aging, to be enjoyed for what it is.

A brick red-orange color on the edge tells that it is a grandfather, to also be enjoyed for what it is, a very mellow and somewhat austere wine, not unlike your grandfather, perhaps.

In general, the older red wines are, the lighter their color, unless they have gone over the top and spoiled, which will be dreadfully evident. At each stage, these older and lighter colored red wines are completely enjoyable, but for different reasons (and with different food, if you are doing the delightful food and wine thing).

The exact opposite is generally true of white wines. With some notable exceptions, mainly in sweet late-harvest or dessert wines such as true sauternes, sherry, and German specialties, the darker the wine becomes, the less enjoyable it becomes. Like red wines, this too is the action of oxygen—oxidation—on wine, but its effects are more harsh on white wines, which lack the tannins and strong flavors to combine with the oxygen, resulting in the white wines tasting distinctly oxidized.

If you want to taste oxidized white wine without ruining a good glass of your special stash, buy a bottle of sherry, the real stuff from Spain. It isn't expensive. Open it and do a sensory test on it. Sherry is wine that is intentionally oxidized, with a lot of alcohol and sweetness added. The purpose of this little experiment is to get you to smell and taste the oxidation so you will remember what oxidized white wine smells and tastes like, not to invite you to drink the whole bottle of sherry. If you have done that, class is over for you for now.

Please don't drive anywhere.

8

Why don't all cabernet sauvignons taste the same?

8

Why don't all cabernet sauvignons taste the same?

When I've asked novice wine drinkers what they really wanted to know about wine, my CPA responded, "Why does your cabernet sauvignon taste different than another one I buy at the market? If I buy two different chocolate bars, two different cartons of milk, two different loaves of white bread, or two different pounds of coffee, they taste pretty much the same. Why is wine different?"

First of all, two different kinds of each of those

things do not taste the same at all. He was just not paying attention to those things as well as I have taught him to pay attention when he tastes my wine. But to address the substance of the question: it's all about the grapes—where they were grown, how they were grown, when they were harvested, and the way the winemaker processes them. If you took a small, level cabernet sauvignon (or zinfandel, pinot noir, or chardonnay) vineyard and divided it in half, picked all the grapes at the same time, and gave half to two different winemakers, the resulting wines would taste different. Guaranteed.

The reason is that there are so many variables in the processing of grapes into wine, and most of them will significantly affect the taste of the final product. To name just a few: the size and gentleness of the crusher that removes the grapes from the stems and breaks the skins; the kind of yeast used to inoculate for fermentation (or if the fermentation is allowed to proceed on "wild" or natural yeasts that live in the vineyard); the temperature of the fermentation; the amount of time the juice is allowed to remain in contact with the stems; how hard the **must,** the mixture of skins, seeds, and fermenting grape juice, is pressed to remove the wine; the type of press; and the size and type of oak (or other material) container in which the wine may be aged.

Is that enough information to give you an idea of the differences in winemaking process? Believe me, there are hundreds more variables. That is what makes a winemaker an artist as well as a scientist. In the same way that a painter can take his basic variables of red, yellow, and blue and make literally millions of shades of color, so does a winemaker have the ability to use his basic variables and produce a wine that has different flavors and aromas.

The winemakers who are good at this make very interesting wines, usually in small batches. When a winemaker starts working with tens of thousands of gallons at once, his job becomes less artistic and more like chemical engineering. The resulting wines are the mass-produced bottles you can purchase at your discount wine stores, grocery retailers, and big box stores for $5.99 and often less.

That is not to say these are undrinkable wines. Plenty of people drink them, and often. But to expect the same tasting or drinking experience from a mass-produced wine as from an artisan-crafted wine is not realistic. You should drink what you like and what you can afford within the boundaries of a guiding principle, unchanged for me since I first imbibed of the grape: "life is too short to drink bad wine."

Only you know what "bad wine" means to you. I have poured down the sink many bottles my CPA would have willingly consumed. This brings me to a warning I feel I should make:

WARNING:
It's difficult to go back to ordinary wines
once you have had the good stuff.

9

Oak in wines

9

Oak in wines

As you read the last chapter, you learned that one of the arrows a winemaker has in his creative quiver is aging wine in oak containers. Traditionally, in most wineries, you will find 225-liter (60-gallon) oak barrels in a couple of styles filled with wine. Several things are going on in that barrel simultaneously:

1. Oxidation

A very small amount of oxygen works its way through the cells of the wood, causing the wine to age. In other words, this process "smoothes out the wine's sharp edges," which is another way of saying oxidize, a term you learned that can be associated with yucky wine if the process is allowed to occur unchecked (i.e., the barrel is left open for a month when the **bung** has popped out unnoticed).

2. Racking

As the wine is clarifying, minute particles of grape solids and yeast cells fall to the bottom of the barrel due to gravity. The resulting sediment is separated from the wine when the wine is **racked.** Racking is the act of removing the wine from the barrel, leaving behind the sediment known as "lees"; washing out the barrel; and returning the wine to its oak home. Tartrates may also fall out as sediment, depending on the temperature and the wine's chemistry, acidity, and other factors.

3. Evaporation

Evaporation also occurs and makes the wine

more concentrated. Depending on the relative humidity, either alcohol or water is working its way out of the barrel. This happens at the rate of about five gallons per barrel per year. This evaporation is known as the "angel's share," a poetic way to rationalize an approximate 10 percent per-year loss per barrel of an expensive product.

4. Picking up oak flavor

The wine picks up oak flavor—oak tannins and vanillin—from the wood of the barrel, adding a dimension of taste to the wine. Sometimes just a little makes a huge difference in the taste. Unless it is overdone, the oak taste is less pronounced in a red wine than in a white wine, in which the lack of other flavors can make the oak stand out. So a winemaker has to be careful not to overdo it, lest consumers be picking oak splinters out of their tongue (I am joking).

Most barrels are made from French oak and American oak. They have different flavors, the American (mostly from Missouri oak) tasting stronger and the French (from, as you may have guessed, French oak forests) more subtle and less astringent.

It is a matter of the winemaker's taste and budget whether she chooses to use French or American. New American barrels of highest quality cost about $350, while French, depending on the euro's exchange rate, cost about $600. I like American oak in reds and French oak in whites.

To further complicate matters, the amount of oak a wine receives depends on a couple of things: the size of the container and the age of the container. A small container has a smaller inside surface-area-to-volume-of-wine ratio than a larger one, and therefore picks up oak flavor more quickly. We know most barrels are about 60 gallons, but in a modern winery, you may find a puncheon, which comes in two sizes, about 80 gallons and about 132 gallons. These are used if the wine doesn't really benefit from oak, or the winemaker has a reason to control the oak extraction.

Some German wine casks I have seen are big enough to store several garbage trucks comfortably. Again, because of their size, very little oak flavor makes its way into the wine. German wines, mostly white, traditionally receive little or no oak addition.

Besides size, the age of the container, or more accurately, how long wine has been stored in it, also affects the level of oak in the aged wine. If you fill a new barrel with wine, it extracts oak flavor quickly because there is a lot of it to be extracted. As the barrel is used year after year, less flavor is available, until an old barrel (three to five years) is considered a neutral storage container. If cared for, a barrel will last a long time. My oldest barrel is about 18 years old and still storing wine, but the wine's not picking up any oak flavor.

At about $600 per French oak barrel (empty!) and around $350 per new American barrel from a wine-barrel maker, you might think there would be a way around this expense. You'd be right. There are a couple of ways commonly used, and I doubt even the most sophisticated palate could tell the difference between these money savers and the money gobblers.

One way is to cut prepared and air-dried French or American oak planks and install them in a tank, fill the tank up with wine, and extract the oak (see StaVin.com for details).

A more common method and one home winemakers use often is to purchase oak chips and add them to the wine. If the wine is stored in a neutral wood container and benefits from the aging, this works very well.

If you have wine experience, you know a very small amount of French white wine has been, for the most part, not "oaked." When French customers taste my chardonnay, which has no new oak contact, they are thrilled to finally experience an American chardonnay that tastes like one with which they are familiar.

So why do winemakers here use so much oak in white wines? I have a theory that the drive to maximize corporate profits leads to **over-cropping,** growing as many grapes per acre as possible, which results in something that can legally be called chardonnay, but which has almost no flavor. Faced with flavorless chardonnay, winemakers use two arrows in their quiver, oak flavor and malolactic butter, to legally add to the flavor profile so the wine has at least some taste. This has, unfortunately, become the American chardonnay style; chardonnay made without oak and malolactic butter needs to be explained to puzzled American consumers, many of whom have literally never tasted anything like it before.

There is an inherent conflict between the grape grower and the quality-minded winemaker. The grower, who gets paid by the ton for grapes, wants maximum yield, and the winemaker desires satisfaction and a reputation by making distinctive wines from low-yield vineyards. There is no regulation in the U.S. about how much yield is allowed per acre. There are regulations in other countries, but I am not an advocate of that sort of interference. Let the market decide. I think you can easily see now why low-yield wines are more expensive.

10

Sediment

10

Sediment

It's easy to tell the neophyte wine drinkers from the ones who have been around the block. The neophytes seem terrified by anything but an absolutely crystal-clear glass of wine; the experienced enthusiasts actually like to see sediment in their bottles. To them it means that the wine has not been overprocessed with fining agents, chemicals, or enzymes. Here's a good example.

Tartaric acid is one of several naturally-occurring

acids in wine. When the wine ages, or is very cold for long enough (i.e., being left in your refrigerator for a week), the tartaric acid precipitates as a solid crystal, potassium bitartrate. Wine tartrate is the exact same thing. Yet this knowledge seems to elude consumers. A customer came into my tasting room carrying an empty bottle of my chardonnay, shouting, "There was glass in my wine!" After calming her down, I showed her that the tartrate crystals were in fact harmless, and I chewed on some to demonstrate the accuracy of my statement.

How can this be prevented? The winemaker drops the temperature in the wine tank to freezing for several days and lets the tartrates fall out in the tank. When the wine is removed, the crystals remain. This process not only makes the wine **cold stable,** but its residual tartrates are also the source of commercial cream of tartar you may have in your spice cabinet. But it takes a very expensive specialized piece of refrigeration equipment and tons of energy to accomplish this cold stabilization. It just doesn't seem worth the effort.

Dark red wine sediment, which clings to the inside of the bottle and is evident on the cork when you pull it (watch out, don't get that on your white shirt, blouse, or tablecloth!), is actually the color molecules in the wine breaking up over time and falling out as a precipitate. As you pour wine with this sediment clinging to the bottle sides, the sediment generally stays put for the first glass. The second and third glasses get cloudy due to the washing back and forth of the liquid as the bottle is tipped. This is one of the reasons we **decant** wine into a decanter or carafe. Decanting is purely an exercise in presenting the wine as clear as you may deem necessary. Wine with some sediment in it tastes the same as the first glass out of the bottle when there is no sediment.

Sediment generally adheres to the sides and top of the bottle because wine is stored on its side to keep the cork from drying out, and it also spends much of its life upside down in a cardboard case of 12 bottles (hence the sediment on the inside of the top and cork).

To **decant for sediment,** you need a clean vessel to receive the clear wine. This can be an expensive crystal decanter for your table, a simple carafe, or even a clean mason jar. In a pinch, I've used a clean vase and even another clean wine bottle with a funnel. My son calls this "MacGyvering it." And it works.

Remove the cork, being careful not to jerk the bottle and dislodge the sediment. Then slowly tip the bottle to the lip of your container. I like to set a bright light under the bottle so that I am looking down through the bottle at the light—LED flashlights are perfect for this and work better than the traditional candle. Keeping the flow slow but steady, you will reach a point where you see a stream of sediment flowing towards your bottle neck. When it gets close, stand the bottle up, stopping the flow. You should have less than a half glass of murky wine in the original bottle and clear wine in your decanting receptacle.

It takes practice to decant successfully for sediment, but the price for messing up is not significant. After decanting, you should make sure to pour the small amount of leftover murky wine into a glass and set it aside while you drink the rest. When you are done with your decanted bottle, the murky wine in the glass may have cleared. And you should drink it, particularly if it is aged fine red wine, the only reason you'd go through the trouble to decant for sediment in the first place.

So, sediment is a natural part of the aging process, not something that is to be confused with spoilage. Very few organisms can live in wine; it has a high acidity and an alcoholic environment (if that sounds like your mother-in-law, I'm sorry for you). That environment is so hostile that pathogens cannot live there, and from that perspective, wine is safe to drink, which is more than you can say about water. It's one of the reasons wine, in all its forms, has been around as long as it has.

The other reason to decant wine is to incorporate air, which is advisable if you are serving a young red wine (up to five years from the vintage date). You should check, but a young red wine generally won't have much sediment in it. **Decanting for air** is much easier than decanting for sediment.

Winemakers spend most of their time doing two things: sanitizing equipment to avoid infestation by unwanted microorganisms, and keeping air away from their wine. A little bit of air makes wine mature and mellow after it is bottled, but a lot of air can trigger spoilage and oxidize the wine. And it's that "little bit of air" that I am interested in telling you about because it can have a profound effect on your enjoyment of a bottle of well-made but young wine.

Most wineries are financially unable to hold their

wines in storage and release them only when they are fully bottle aged and at their peak of perfection. And the smaller wineries that are producing high-quality red wines are the ones that can least afford to hold on to their inventory before releasing it. So, my friend, that $52 bottle of recent vintage cabernet sauvignon you bought for your anniversary dinner may be excellent in quality, but there is a good chance it will be much more ready to drink eight to twelve months from now. If you taste it and the words "tight" and "astringent" seem to apply more than "open" and "smooth," here is what you need to do.

If you have a wine decanter, wash it out. If you find yourself decanterless, use a very clean flower vase or other similar container. Take your bottle of wine and upend it into the container, making sure it splashes and foams. Get air into it. Then leave the red wine alone for several minutes, perhaps while you have your first course, which will likely take a white wine.

When you retaste your young cabernet, you should find it much more approachable and drinkable with rounder edges. In effect, you have aged the wine in the decanter by adding air to the wine, allowing it not only to breathe, but also to gulp in great quantities of oxygen. In the next twenty minutes, it will taste significantly smoother.

11

Sulfites:
what's the big deal?

11

Sulfites: what's the big deal?

Let's start here: **sulfites** occur naturally as a minor by-product of fermentation—not much, about 8 parts per million (ppm). That is about 2 1/2 teaspoons in 264 gallons, which is hard to visualize. Think of a 55-gallon drum. Then think of five of them and put your 2 1/2 teaspoons in that. Eight parts per million, not very much.

The winemaker adds sulfite to wine mainly to protect it against oxidation. When wine comes into contact with oxygen where sulfite is present, the oxygen combines first with the sulfite. When the sulfite is all used up, the oxygen combines with the wine's components, forming aldehydes and other compounds, causing it to smell and taste nasty.

Federal regulations allow the addition of up to 350 ppm (about 2.27 cups in the same five 55 gallon drums), but that is a very high level, and a level at which you might start tasting sulfite in your wine. So most wineries use far less than 350 ppm.

It is possible to make and bottle wine without sulfites. Several wineries do just that. But if these wines are palatable when they went into the bottles, you need to drink them young, before the small amount of oxygen introduced during sterile filtration and bottling (even if that's done in a nitrogen environment) has its way with the wine.

I often speak with people who have traveled to Italy and say something like this:

Person: "I just got back from (region in Italy) and we drank a lot of red wine all the time, and I never got a headache or had any problems."

Me: "Why do you think that is the case?"

Person: "Oh, I heard they don't use any sulfites in

their wines."

Me: " Yes, they do, but their government doesn't make them put that on the label."

Me: "Additionally, most Italian wines are made from varietals that have light bodies, fewer tannins, and a lot less alcohol than U.S.–made wines. Thus, consumption results in fewer reactions to those components, especially when excessive consumption occurs."

Why are we required to put that government warning and the sulfite warning on all labels sold in the U.S.? Because in the heyday of salad bars, lettuce and salad items were sprayed with highly concentrated sulfite so that they would not oxidize and turn brown. Eventually, a very small number of people started to notice an allergic reaction to the salads and upon discovery of the culprit sulfite, they raised a hue and alarm such as you never heard before. The government response was, without regard to concentration, to slap a warning label on wine. I have never seen a similar warning on a salad bar, concentrated orange juice, or dried fruit, items in which sulfite is commonly used.

There is no scientific proof that sulfite causes

headaches. If you think it does, eat some orange colored dried apricots (which contain far more sulfite than any wine you will ever drink) and see if you get a pounder. Then contact Dr. Andrew L. Waterhouse at UC Davis (http://waterhouse.ucdavis.edu/wine-comp/so2.htm) so you can take part in a controlled experiment that will verify the truth.

Headaches from excessive red wine consumption are caused by your body's reaction to tannins, alcohol, sugar, and dehydration (red wine is a diuretic). If you drink a lot of water while consuming wine and other alcoholic beverages, you will be less likely to suffer from a headache. Ever notice that beer drinkers may have bodily complaints, but a headache is not one of them, at least if they have been drinking only beer and not boilermakers? It may be caused by the water-to-alcohol ratio that is inherent in beer (see Chapter 22, Water into wine).

12

Cork conflict

12

Cork conflict

That little piece of bark—yes, cork is bark harvested from a kind of oak tree—is the focus of
much controversy among today's winemakers. Here
at my winery, we think there is something more to
the discussion than substituting cork with alternative closures as a quality issue.

Proponents of alternative closures beat on the
drum of **TCA**, or trichloroanisole, the chemical
produced by certain molds that in the presence of

chlorine give corked wine its spoiled, wet cardboard smell. Some say as much as 8 percent of all wine is infested with this disgusting smell, but I believe that figure is grossly overstated. I have been making wine since 1974, commercially since 1987, have pulled countless corks here in the tasting room or at home, and have smelled each one of them. I can count the **"corked"** wines on one hand. What is true is that some people are much more sensitive to the smell than others, so I have a small bottle of TCA on hand if customers feel they'd like to educate their nose palate to the smell. It's pretty terrible, and I'd bet you'd never forget it once you got a nose full.

The reaction to this TCA "problem" was to switch to a different closure. I believe the popularity of plastic substitutes or even screw-top closures is based in cost savings as much as any other factor. It is a decision made by the corporate controller, who, as wineries look more and more like refineries, is responsible for assuring the corporation's financial quality.

A decent 1 3/4" cork cost about 30 cents. If you buy 100,000 of them, the price doesn't drop significantly. I recently received a quote from a supplier for the same sized plastic cork at 11.8 cents each. Eighteen cents difference doesn't seem like much, unless you are bottling twenty million bottles; then the difference would pay plenty of hungry stockholders. And if you bought twenty million artificial closures, you'd get an extremely good price; all the manufacturer has to do is turn on the extruder to form the plastic closures. Of course, all those twenty million pieces of petroleum-based plastic will become part of our landfills.

On the other hand, natural cork is truly a renewable resource. It takes a twenty-five-year-old cork tree, usually grown in Spain and Portugal, from seven to nine years to develop a new bark to be made into corks. And even though winery names print very cleanly and nicely on plastic closures, any closure is part of the aesthetic and tradition of the entire product. And if wine is anything, it is traditional.

The screw top is a piece of aluminum formed to fit on a specific bottle. This is a very acceptable closure for a young white wine that is going to be consumed very soon after bottling. Light whites from New Zealand and Australia are wines that fit this model perfectly. But when I see "name" wineries releasing big, tannic, age-requiring red wines in this package, I smile my corporate-controller smile.

Back to the idea of wine as traditional, it is hard to imagine a young lover opening a bottle of wine under the arbor on an idyllic, warm, sunny afternoon, and instead of the "pop" of a cork that precedes the clinking of glasses, to hear a "crack" as the screw-top seal is broken. But then, I'm a romantic. I like to say that when Chateau Petrus starts using artificial closures, I will consider it. Until then, I'll stick with natural cork.

Oddly, in my opinion, the best non-cork closure for wine is the one associated with cheap **plonk,** a term you should know is not a very nice thing to say about a wine. The closure I am referring to is the bag-in-a-box container. Usually you can find these wine boxes on the shelf at your local megamart drugstore at a price less than that of bottled water. The container is great for wine because the flexible bag inside the box is constructed of multilayered foil and plastic designed to be an oxygen barrier. The bag collapses as the wine is released through a shutoff valve, so there is no air contact. Effective and cheap, this is a perfect system for everyday table wine. Because it is associated with the low-end brands, it may never have the chance to package better wines.

I'll say it again. Wine is nothing if not traditional.

And the pulling of a natural cork, while perhaps not as convenient as or as inexpensive as the boxed bag or the screw top, is a part of the centuries-old wine experience.

13
Corked wine and TCA

13

Corked wine and TCA

You learned a little about corked wine in the last chapter, but the subject warrants even closer inspection. At some point, you will hear someone say, "This wine is corked." And when they hand you the glass, it will be revealing if you know what to do.

Don't take the glass. Ask to see the cork so that you can smell it, for it is from the cork that the moldy, wet cardboard smell emanates, and once it migrates to the wine, the effect is much more subtle.

In fact, I'd go so far as to say that most people would drink a glass of corked wine and be none the wiser. As you learn to taste wine and focus your senses, the off-smell of corked wine should be obvious to you. Remember the difference between drinking and tasting wine.

I smell every cork I pull as an automatic part of operating the corkscrew. It takes less than a second. If you smell something that reminds you of what a wet cardboard box would smell like, only stronger, you probably have some TCA spoilage in the wine. Different people have different levels of sensitivity to this chemical, so don't immediately dump the bottle. Sometimes older red wine smells a little musty or earthy (you might smell a little musty, too, if you'd been locked up in a bottle for ten years). These odors are volatile and will usually blow off once the wine is in the glass.

If you smell the cork and the smell rocks your head back as if you'd been slapped, you probably have a corked wine infected with TCA, trichloranisole. No, you don't need to memorize that; TCA is enough.

If the wine in your glass lacks fruit and there is really no bouquet except for that faint, wet cardboard smell, you may decide to serve the wine to your drinking friends who are chugging red wine with their pepperoni pizza anyway. TCA will not harm you in the concentrations you will experience in a tainted bottle of wine.

The truth is, you may go through your entire wine-tasting life and never experience a corked bottle. The cork industry got its act together and has changed practices to eliminate the TCA threat. So no longer will you find the forest worker peeling the bark from a cork tree and laying it on the spore-infested forest floor, then moving on to the next tree. Corks are now sanitized and lightened with hydrogen peroxide instead of chlorine bleach.

The industry, once threatened by replacement closures, has regained the confidence of winemakers and consumers alike. So unless you open ten or twenty bottles a day, the odds of you experiencing TCA are slim.

14

ML (malolactic) fermentation

14

ML (malolactic) fermentation

Malolactic fermentation (or ML for short) is another arrow in the winemaker's quiver for her to hit the style target for which she's aiming.

To keep this easily understandable, the ML fermentation is usually accomplished after the sugar fermentation by bacteria rather than yeast. These bacteria are everywhere; you probably have ten million of them on your nose right now. The bacteria have the ability to act on malic acid, a natural organic acid found in wine grapes, the same acid found in green apples. The bacteria converts the **malic acid** to **lactic acid,** the acid found in milk products. Think of biting into a green apple. It's tart, sour, zingy, and strong. Now think of the acid taste in milk. It's softer, lighter, smoother, and more pleasant. That's exactly what is happening to a wine undergoing ML fermentation.

Chardonnay is a good example of what happens to white wine undergoing ML. Chardonnay is a grape that tastes fairly neutral to start with. If over-cropped, it is even more neutral. In order to give the wine some flavor, it is often run through an oak barrel then encouraged to go through ML fermentation. The lactic acid changes the flavor to a softer, rounder wine with a distinct buttery flavor. A glass of this wine is enjoyed before dinner, perhaps sitting on your deck.

Wine from low-yield chardonnay grapes that have a more intense flavor can be prevented from going through ML, and the resulting wine (i.e., French-style chardonnay) has a crisp, acidic flavor often reminiscent of apples. This style of chardonnay is matched to food, particularly richer, fattier foods with sauces.

Preventing ML fermentation is sometimes difficult. Most big wineries sterile filter their wines so that ML does not happen in the bottle, causing cloudiness and gas bubbles, something the mass-market audience will not tolerate. Smaller wineries can safely prevent ML by keeping the wine high in acidity, low in temperature, at proper sulfite levels, and at high enough alcohol levels. Even so, artisan wines may go through partial ML because artisan winemakers are loathe to sterile filter their wines, believing that it leaves their wines stripped completely and lifeless.

15

Sweet wines and the wine cycle

15

Sweet wines and the wine cycle

Some wine aficionados look down upon sweet wine and sweet wine drinkers as less sophisticated than the aficionado. The truth is that that same aficionado probably started his or her wine drinking as a consumer of sweet wines. And we Americans particularly like sweet foods and drinks.

A primal human urge is to seek out things that taste good and avoid things that taste bad. Sugar tastes good and is favored because we as human organisms need calories to supply energy to not just our muscles but also to that CPU between our ears. That computer is running our entire system on glucose; no sugar, and—system failure!—we have to reboot.

It's not easy for a winemaker to simply stop the fermentation of a wine and leave a little **residual sugar,** or **RS,** in it because the yeast that ferments the sugar into alcohol is a persistent little bug. Even when a wine has been protected against all re-fermentation, unless it has been sterile filtered, some yeast will persist, and continued fermentation will likely take place when conditions are ripe (higher temperature, lower sulfite levels). A wine produced in this manner will generally have a lower alcohol percentage than most wines because the sugar that remains in the wine was not fermented into alcohol. Take a close look at the alcohol level in a normal German Riesling. Unless it was fermented to dryness, a Riesling usually has an RS of 1 to 3 percent. The Riesling alcohol totals to about 8 to 10 percent, which is lower than a dry wine (no sugar left).

A dessert wine with more than 1 percent sugar has probably been processed to remove all the yeast cells, or else it has been **fortified.** Fortification is the addition of high proof spirits (alcohol) to the wine in order to raise the level of the alcohol past the point at which yeast can live. If you look at the label of a bottle of real port, you will see its alcohol level is about 20 percent. The winemaker uses yeast in the base wine that will not survive that level of alcohol, and so the fermentation stops with sugar remaining.

Dessert wines can be lovely and expensive. A half bottle of top-of-the-line German Riesling can easily cost $100. But wait—before you rush out to buy a case, you need to know a basic truth about serving sweet wines.

If you are serving a sweet wine with a dessert, the wine must be sweeter than the dish you are serving with it. One of the most magnificent pairings is dark chocolate and an aged ruby port, a marriage made in heaven. Change out the dark chocolate for milk chocolate, which contains lots of sugar, and the marriage falls apart because the sugar in the chocolate makes the port taste sour. This is the same principle you learned in the tasting order of wines: start with light wines, move to heavier wines, then to sweet wines. Never move from sweet wines to dry wines, or the dry wines will be sour to your palate.

Most people who like sweet wines generally do

not drink port or other fortified wines, but rather white wines that contain a small amount of sugar (1 to 3 percent). In large part, these are made by big wineries with large distribution arms that reach into your supermarket, and plenty of filtration equipment on hand to filter out all traces of yeast.

My father is one of those sweet wine people. He just didn't like dry wines and insisted on a white wine I will not name here, but it had plenty of sugar to tame his wild sweet tooth. He was caught in the first part of his wine cycle. I believe that most wine consumers follow a definite pattern as they experience wine over time. As a young adult attracted to sweetness, the wine of choice becomes a sweet blush wine or a wine with some perceptible RS. If the person explores, he moves on to dry white wines with flavor and structure. Oaked, buttery chardonnay fits this niche. With a little more exposure, it's on to light and fruity reds, Italian varietals, gamay, pinot noir, then heavier, full-bodied reds (zinfandel, syrah, cabernet sauvignon) and then full circle back to sweet with an attraction to complex port, sauternes, sherry, and marsala. That full circle is what I call the wine cycle, and where you are on it tells volumes about what you have been drinking and what you have yet to experience.

Yes, people's tastes change, and without consciously making a change to the next step, you may find yourself deep in your current position on the cycle, enjoying all the new sensations and flavors. This is part of the reason it is so important to be open-minded and willing to try just about any wine placed before you. I only draw the wine at retsina, a pine-pitch-flavored wine from Greece, but I did try it. Once.

16

All about wine snobs

16

All about wine snobs

We said that the first part of this book was going to be about what wine is and the second part was going to be about how to enjoy it. We are just about at that tipping point. If you have been paying attention, you know quite a bit about what wine is, way more than your average friend.

The name "wine snob" is pejorative nomenclature. It is not quite as high on the insult scale as some expletives but higher than "jerk," and it is not a term you want people to associate with you. So, here is some advice. The difference between "that person is very knowledgeable about wine" and "that guy's a wine snob" is all in how the information in one's knowledge base is delivered.

If you start throwing terms around the wine bar, "RS this" and "ML that," people are going to have a negative reaction toward you. Oh, there might be a star-crossed young thing who thinks that your knowledge is very attractive, but he or she will probably be allowed to drink only soda pop.

Behavior and tone is very important in avoiding the wine snob tag. Some people who are, shall we say, insecure and defensive, are going to call you a cork dork or a wine snob just because you know more than they do about the subject. Let's set those people up to succeed by prefacing our comments with something like this: "I read in Paul Kreider's book that wines can have sugar left in them, and this one tastes sweet to me. Can you tell me whether it has residual sugar?" Whoever is selling the wine should know the percentage. Contrast that delivery with "What's the RS of this wine?" and you will see why you might get a different response, not just from the person behind the bar, but from those on your side of it as well.

Present yourself as a student, and people will be willing to teach you. "I'm learning about malolactic fermentation; has this chardonnay been through it?" In a way, you are disclosing your knowledge by asking the question. The answer is less important because you already know the answer and are letting someone else display their knowledge.

"That dryness in my mouth when I taste this syrah, that cotton feeling on my tongue—is that what you call tannins?"

The need to assert your ego is painfully evident when you pour the wine into the dump bucket and say, "Too tannic." Not cool.

People whom you have called wine snobs in the past because they demonstrated the knowledge you lacked may easily be your wine-tasting friends in the future. See if the knowledge you are achieving changes your attitude about them.

A different kind of wine snob and one who has a completely different problem is someone who defines his wine collection by what it cost.

There is plenty of room in the wine experience for someone to brag about their $1200 bottle of chateau petrus, their $250 bottle of Napa cabernet, or even their $100 bottle of special chardonnay. These people are equating the price they paid with the quality of their collection. And we do know there is a correlation between price and quality, but at the extremes of the $1200 bottle, it is more about the scarcity of the product than the quality of the wines. Yes, expensive wines should be good, or there would not be a market for them in the first place. When 10,000 customers are after 1,000 bottles, it drives the price up. So what your friend is bragging about is that he has a lot of disposable income. How attractive is that?

17
Smelling and tasting

17

Smelling and tasting

If you can't smell, you can't taste. I have performed this smell-taste exercise in my wine appreciation classes, and you can try it at home. You don't need to be a professional.

I pour each participant a couple of ounces of colorless flavored soft drink and make sure that the glass is far enough across the table from them that they cannot smell it. I then instruct each person to drink half of it while holding her nose. What flavor is it? Maybe the participant will sense a little acid, but no flavors. I then tell them to release their hands from their noses, breathe normally, and drink the other half. This time, the flavor is obvious.

Did your parent ever tell you at the dinner table to chew with your mouth shut? Well, why was the child chewing with his mouth open in the first place? Because taking air in with your food allows you to smell and taste it with the taste buds that are not just in your mouth, but all the way up the back of your nasal cavity. Food tastes better and more intense to both you and your child when it is supplemented by air.

Now you know why wine tasters make that funny slurping sound when they have wine in their mouths. They are sucking air in through the wine to gain the most intense senses of that sip. Remember, they are tasting, not drinking, the wine. You should try this aeration at home, too, because it does take some practice. I'd rather you cough wine all over your kitchen table than all over the waiter and your date at your local linen tablecloth and silver restaurant.

Start off slowly. Take a sip of wine and as or just before you swallow it, breathe in a little burst of air and notice how that changes things on your palate. After you have mastered this wine bump, try pulling air in through the wine you hold in the front of your mouth. Do this with a slurping action that leaves the wine in the front with you pulling air bubbles through your mouth. Then swallow it, continuing to draw in air. See how different that makes it taste? You should sense different layers of flavors and sensations.

At the point your palate fails to respond to the differences among wines (for me, it's after about seven tastings), you are experiencing **palate fatigue,** meaning you have overloaded and deadened your taste-bud receptors and need to take a break. Sometimes eating a piece of plain bread or an unflavored breadstick, water cracker, or other bland snack will do the trick. It should now be obvious why tasting wine when you have a cold is a waste of time and wine. Other no-nos in wine-tasting environments are chewing gum, wearing perfumes, eating mints, and drinking coffee.

Describing a wine's tastes and smells is what the whole experience is about, and communicating about the flavors and smells takes experience. Do it over and over with the same wine and with different ones. Rest assured that your sense of smell and taste are very strong, long-lasting, memorable, and influential. Perfume and cologne manufactures count on it—the whiff of a certain perfume vividly reminds you of a person you have not seen in years. Or the aroma of chocolate chip cookies brings you right back to your grandmother's kitchen. So eventually will that plum, blackberry aroma and that black pepper tang make you recall a zinfandel you had in a large bowled glass ten years ago. The ability to accurately remember smells and tastes is hardwired into your DNA. All you need to do is pay attention.

While we are talking about physiology, let me bring another aspect to the conversation. Have you ever been cooking an herb-rich dish and remark upon how good it smells, only to discover that twenty minutes later you don't smell it anymore? Or perhaps you leave the house to do something and return to rediscover the wonderful smells you had first experienced? Why did you lose it? **Olfactory fatigue.** Your olfactory receptors are prone to tire. Too much of anything shuts them down. The perfume or cologne you wear smells great when you apply it but disappears from your sensory map in twenty minutes or less for the same reason. Ever wonder how people can live next to a smelly dump or factory? They literally don't smell it.

Once, driving in an open vehicle through the German countryside, I came upon a farmhouse with a huge pile of manure-laden hay next to it. It smelled so badly of ammonia my eyes watered. I learned that the farmer used this to fertilize the fields, and I know he could sleep in his house right next to it only because his olfactory sensors were down for the count.

So the lesson here is to enjoy wine's smells and tastes, but realize that you will do that best with some air mixed in. At one point in the session, you will experience a lessening of your perception or enjoyment because of fatigue.

18

Enjoying wine by using a thermometer

18

Enjoying wine by
using a thermometer

This chapter is not meant to encourage you to
rush around like a scientist with an instant-read
thermometer (although I do have one in my kitch-
en that is pretty cool). What I want you to grasp is
that, in the words of a visitor from Europe: "Americans drink their red wines too warm and their white
wines too cold." I could not agree with him more,
particularly about the whites.

As a winemaker, it is frustrating to go to a casual

party or to a restaurant and see a bottle of chardonnay I know to have great fruit acidity and balance, stuck in a bucket filled with ice and water. (They are called *champagne* buckets for a reason!) At that temperature, a still white wine tastes like cold liquid, with little to distinguish it from ice water except the alcohol hit. Sparkling wine and champagne are different—they're less about the fruit and bouquet and more about the bubbles. Colder is better and retains the bubbles.

White wines should be served cool at about 45 degrees Fahrenheit, not cold. My refrigerator wine measures 38 degrees Fahrenheit. This means that if you have a nice bottle of white in your fridge that you want to serve to dinner guests, remove it from the fridge and set it on the counter for fifteen minutes before you serve it. Assuming the counter isn't at 120 degrees, in fifteen minutes the wine should be close to 45 degrees Fahrenheit. Better yet, open the wine taken from the refrigerator and taste a little, then taste some at fifteen minutes. You will experience all the bouquet and volatile aromas you can't get to when the wine is too cold.

Red wines are a little different. Drunk too cold, as in out of a cold wine cellar or—more likely—out of your car parked overnight in the snow, all you are going to taste is alcohol and tannins. "Serve at room temperature" doesn't do much for us in the twenty-first century in the U.S., and was perhaps a better temperature indicator in Europe in the early twentieth century before central heating and climate-controlled chateaux. I'm a fan of 68 degrees Fahrenheit because that is the temperature at which the dry reds taste best to me. You need to determine what is best for you. You can do this by tasting a wine you are storing in your living room at somewhere in the low 70s, then corking it and putting it in your refrigerator for ten minutes and tasting it again.

Obviously, how long you are cooling your reds or warming your whites depends on your starting temperatures. Remember that the 45 degrees Fahrenheit for white and the 68 degrees Fahrenheit for red are approximate drinking points, not something written in concrete. But when you taste the same wine side by side at different temperatures, you will be a believer in carrying a thermometer in your pocket.

19

Getting the data to your receptors

19

Getting the data to your receptors

It is all very good to talk about olfactory taste-bud receptors you use during a wine-tasting session (I didn't want to alarm you in the previous chapter; this part of the tasting process is known as the "**organoleptic evaluation**"). But just how do you get the wine to your receptors?

We have discussed that the color of the wine is important, and the best way to observe it is to hold the glass against a white background and look at

the meniscus. Evaluating the smell of a wine—
"bouquet" or **"aroma"** in wine-speak—is a little
more complicated. If you have seen people swirling
their glass a time or two and then sniffing it before
remarking, "Oh, lovely bouquet," do not use that as
your wine-tasting model.

If you really want to experience the aromas of a
wine, you need to start with a proper wine-tasting
glass. These are shaped like a tulip with a wide bottom and rim that is smaller than the bottom. The
bowl is designed for swirling the wine without it fly-
ing all over the room or on your shirt or blouse.

Taking your glass with a small amount of wine in
it, place it on a solid, smooth surface, such as a counter or a wine bar. Grasp the stem close to the base
with your finger and thumb, and pressing down on
the flat surface, twirl the glass like a hula-hoop (even
if it's been forever since you have used or even seen
a hula-hoop).

When you do this properly, the centrifugal force
of the twirling will spin the wine up the sides of the
glass. In short, you will know if your tasting glass is a
proper one. When you have done this hula-hooping
for five or six turns, pick up the glass and stick your
nose in it. Whether your nose is a little button or a

huge honker, it should go into the glass as far as it can. Breathe in. Now you are smelling the wine like a pro.

Notice how strong the various components seem? This is because the inside surface of that glass is not smooth, but has microscopic jagged points protruding from it. As you swirl the wine, these points rip the wine, causing molecules of wine to go into the atmosphere, an atmosphere that is neatly contained in the glass by its small opening. That glass is just waiting for you to sink your nose and attached olfactory receptors into its wonderful cloud.

Caution: many wineglasses, designed for elegant frou-frou dinner service rather than wine appreciation, have a wider mouth than bowl. Do not try this vigorous swirling with one of those kinds of glasses, or you will make an embarrassing mess.

As discussed, the actual wine flavors on your palate are enhanced by air and the drawing up of molecules of wine into your nasal cavity. Practice makes perfect. Part of the key here is to take a very small amount of wine into your mouth rather than a mouthful as if you were washing down a forkful of lasagna.

Focusing your attention on the wine can be difficult because we are all easily distracted—distracted by chatter, a new person entering the room, the server pouring the samples. Another concentration hazard is your propensity to consider suggestions from others. The mind is a powerful thing, and if in the midst of tasting your sample, someone says, "I taste jalapeno in this wine," then by golly, you are going to taste jalapeno in your glass. That is why really serious wine tasting features two characteristics:

1. The participants do not talk; and
2. The wine bottles are in bags so you cannot see the labels.

This is called tasting blind, and it can be set up as a fun event. It's all about focus and the lack of suggestion.

20
Aging wine gracefully

20

Aging wine gracefully

When a zinfandel or merlot (and most sturdy red wine) is young, generally considered to be within one to five years of the vintage date on the bottle, it shows a deep purple color, produces intense fruit flavor in the nose, and is sometimes "hot" when alcohol predominates the taste. It has less overall smoothness than it will show later in its life. As the wine ages, the alcohol, tannic acid (from the grapeskins and the oak in the barrel), and fruit flavors start to soften and blend together to present a more smooth, finished wine. This is called the **integration** of components. Often the differences in taste between young wine and well-aged, integrated wine are extremely evident, so aged wine is sometimes very desirable.

Please note that you, the consumer, have very little control over the many winemaking variables that set up a wine to be a good candidate for aging. But you do have some control over cellar storage conditions that affect aging, namely temperature, light, humidity, and vibration.

In California there are darned few houses built with cellars in them. You can "cellar" a wine in a closet or pay some bucks for a temperature- and humidity-controlled cabinet in which you can store your treasures. If you are interested in and have the personal discipline to cellar some wines over the several years it takes, here is a tip before you start.

Some wine does not get better with age, it just gets older. This is particularly true of most white wines and certainly sparkling wine or champagne. I have shed tears over unopened bottles of excellent French champagne that were saved in a well-intentioned effort from someone's wedding twenty years ago. Champagne is meant to be consumed shortly after it is released and does not improve in the bottle after it is released.

The key to cellaring successfully is to start with something that has the potential to improve. In red wines that usually means a big, well-made, unbalanced and probably expensive cabernet sauvignon, pinot noir, zinfandel, or merlot or port. In whites a really big oaked chardonnay or a very sweet, rich dessert wine such as true Sauternes or a German trockenbeerenauslese can be deemed worthy of the time and expense cellar aging requires.

I am afraid the expensive part of that statement is very true. Cellaring your typical $7 bottle of supermarket zinfandel is going to be a disappointing exercise in patience, but if you are able to purchase some massive, oaky, tannic red (but not high alcohol, which doesn't seem to age well), you will likely have a candidate for aging. What you should look for is something that has a component or components out of balance. Heavy tannins would be something that time could tame.

The most important variable in aging wine is the temperature at which it is stored—not simply the number of degrees, but the *range* of the temperatures. If you had a perfect situation and could hold your wines at 65 degrees Fahrenheit year-round, you would be set. However, if your cellar temperature fluctuates from 50 to 80 degrees Fahrenheit or higher, you may just as well drink it now. What happens with that range is the liquid in the bottle expands and contracts with the temperature and eventually pushes around the cork, breaking the seal and allowing air to enter. This starts a chain reaction of microbial actions. Result: spoiled, expensive old wine and tears of frustration.

Do I need to tell you to store wine on its side so that the cork stays moist and doesn't dry out? If you fail to do this, see the paragraph above, because the result is the same.

Collecting and aging wine takes money, care, time, money, knowledge, and money. If you have all those, it can be a worthwhile and rewarding pursuit. At one point in the not-so-distant past, there were French red wines you simply had to age, as they were literally undrinkable when first released and were purchased by cognoscenti who would not have dreamed of opening them for at least ten years! Such winemaking techniques have mostly faded from the scene, so most wine now is released ready to be splashed into a glass and consumed. If you do find one that could be saved and improved, try to do so for your own education.

21

Class on glass

21

Class on glass

In order to enjoy the impact of this section, you need to understand that I am a person who has sipped more than his share of everyday wine from a rough, dishwasher-scratched Duralex ("Made in France") glass, a glass with all the elegance of a Mason jar. I own fancy stemware for serious tasting, but cleaning it is a bother and expensive, given the burliness of my forearm and the delicate structure of the glass stem. The Duralex, which I first experienced in a brasserie in a town somewhere in France when I was *tres* younger than I am now, had its own special cachet and seemed adequate for most of my normal consumption at dinner. It was easy to hold, nearly unbreakable, fit easily in the dishwasher, stacked easily for storage, and most importantly, did an excellent job of keeping the wine off the tabletop.

You can imagine my reaction when someone told me that the latest of hip wine practices is for patrons to bring their own stemware in a foam-fitted case to restaurants, to better enjoy their wine selections. It was like someone reached up and flipped my boggle switch. It was difficult to take seriously.

Then I was invited to a tasting at a friend's house where wines were served from the same bottle during dinner, right in front of my eyes, one glass in a restaurant clunker (although not Duralex, something that would stand up to lots of dishwasher abuse) and the other serving in a Riedel glass, thin and very well formed for that particular type of wine. So, there was a chardonnay glass and pinot noir glass and zinfandel glass all lined up, each shaped differently. And I was so ready to expose this hoax as just another way for some glass manufacturer to sell more stemware.

I was prepared to focus everything I had on the

smells and flavors in those two different glasses, and I did, and you know what? They were right. The wine was significantly better in the expensive stemware; it had better aroma, looked nicer, and, as I was later told, because the shape caused the wine to spill onto the part of your tongue where its predominant flavor would be most perceptive, tasted a whole lot better. It was the same wine, different level of glass.

In the same way you can take a snapshot out of that messy pile of photographs you have in a drawer somewhere in your house and spend a few dollars on a nice frame, instantly transforming that photo into a masterpiece worthy of your fireplace mantle, so can you frame a wine in a way that draws attention to its uniqueness and most attractive features by spending some money on a special glass.

If the stemware you choose is made lead-free, as most of it is now, you can most likely wash it in your dishwasher. I even wash my delicate and expensive Bottega del Vino (www.bottegadelvinocrystal.com) hand-blown pieces in my commercial dishwasher at the winery. At $50 plus per stem, you may think this is brave, but I have never lost a glass in the dishwasher, only when I was washing them by hand.

Leaded crystal was the standard of excellence for

centuries, but the discovery that long-term storage of high alcohol leaches the lead from the crystal into the liquid pretty much put an end to leaded crystal for scotch and other distilled beverages. It didn't take long for the hyper-paranoid to demand that lead be removed from temporary low-alcohol containers such as wineglasses also. And so now that is the standard. Good thing too. If I had washed my leaded glasses in the dishwasher, the high heat would have turned the glass milky white. Yes, it was another hard-learned lesson.

22

Water into wine

22

Water into wine

Winemakers are known for their craft of making wine from grapes, but they are also very crafty people, cleverly using what is at hand to create whatever is necessary to complete their task. "Resourceful people" would be another way you could phrase it (but it wouldn't make that sentence as much fun as it is).

We hold wine-related dinners in my winery as promotional events after work parties (bottling, crushing, et cetera), and as you might imagine, co-pious amounts of wine are consumed. Many partici-pants are attorneys, and it became apparent there was some liability inherent in allowing people to consume wine at a social function in my winery and then for them to drive away down the street. The same is true in your home, so you should share my concern not only for your friends' safety but for your financial security should something go awry and a tree jump out in front of your impaired pal's car.

Rule Number One is fairly well known, but bears repeating: always serve plenty of food with wine. A stomach with something in it tempers the rate at which alcohol enters the bloodstream and avoids the one-glass-staggering-about-the-room syndrome. Cheese works very well for me, but a rare prime rib roast is preferred.

Rule Number Two, very effective at dinner par-ties where several wines and food are to be served, is to have plenty of water available and keep everyone's water glass filled. Bottled or sparkling water, home-filtered water, or any clean-tasting water will do. Go fancy and place a thin slice of fresh lemon in the glass. As people talk and eat and talk, you will find that if water is available, they will drink it in great gulps, between taking (one hopes) smaller amounts of wine with food. There are several benefits to this strategy of serving water:

1. People will consume water, which is considerably less expensive than wine. (If this does not appear to be true, you may consider changing your brand of bottled water, or your selection of wine, or both.)
2. People will dilute the alcohol level in their system with water and not become as tipsy.
3. Wine, especially red wine, acts as a diuretic, causing dehydration and thirst. By hydrating with water, your guests will avoid the drugged feeling that comes with dehydration and will also feel less of the effects wine causes some people the next morning when alcohol has sucked all the water out of their frontal lobe.

The only negative to this water strategy is that passionate and loquacious conversation will be interrupted as people excuse themselves to use the bathroom frequently. On second thought, maybe that isn't such a big negative.

23

Wine reviewers and point systems

23

Wine reviewers and point systems

The problem with buying wine at a retailer where you cannot taste before laying out your hard-earned green is that when you get the wine home, you may find that it is very different from what you like. This promotes the practice of you buying a national homogenized brand that you know is going to be the same whenever and wherever you buy it and foregoing the unknown labels for fear that you will be wasting money on something you might not like.

This is not unlike the McDonald's hamburger syndrome wherein any place you go in the U.S., one of their hamburgers is going to taste exactly like the one you had at your corner McDonald's back home. That may bring you some level of comfort, but before you know it: homogeneity! All the hamburgers are produced by three or four major franchised producers as identical, cheap, tasty (if not healthy) hamburgers. Although their products may have some minor differences, they are basically the same. You don't want your wine industry to become any more like that than it is already. So try something new!

Start by trying a different producer of a varietal you already know you like. If you like XYZ Winery's Sonoma Valley chardonnay, try ABC Winery's Sonoma Valley chardonnay. The wines should be different, particularly if they are small producers. Branch out and try a chardonnay from a totally different appellation, and then try one from France. Trying new wines is the only way you will develop a deep palate.

If you are timid, there are legions of wine reviewers standing ready to tell you what wines you should like. The newspapers are full of reviewers, and the

Internet only brings more to your attention. All can be a source of good information to help you decide which bottle you should buy next. Does this mean that you should rush to buy wine the reviewer has awarded 95 points or more? You'd be surprised how many people are so unsure of what they like, they do just that. Just remember, wine reviewers are people just like you, who have their own likes and dislikes, favorites and prejudices. Just because this reviewer rates the $68 pinot noir highly and thinks it is great is not a good reason for you to plunk down your child's lunch money for the month to buy a bottle. And it is uncanny how often the reviewer's favorite costs $68 (or more), which make me feel they are out of touch with us common folks' wine-drinking reality. Or maybe they really don't want us to drink it, just covet the stuff.

Once I read a review about a white wine blend from a winery I knew to make distinctive wines. It got a rave review, and I was halfway out the door to locate some when I noticed that the price was $90 per bottle. When I see that, I ask myself, "Would I rather have one bottle of this or three bottles of that excellent (and not inexpensive) $30 white blend I drank last week?" And the answer makes it clear whether I should put my keys back in my pocket.

At one point, you will be able to taste a wine and say to yourself with confidence, "Great nose, wonderful fruit, well structured, long finish. This is what I want!" and when you can do that, you won't need anybody to tell you what is good, just use them to point you in the right direction.

If you do find a reviewer whose perspective seems to mesh with yours, become a fan and be vocal about it to everyone you meet and to the publication in which the reviews appear. This will help assure that the reviewer stays in reviewing and that your source of valued information will continue to provide it.

Another source of information about the wine you may purchase is the staff at the store where you would buy it. However, there seems to be an inverse relationship between the size of the shop and the level of information the staff can dispense. Your mega bottle store usually employs clerks, and the local bottle shop usually employs or is run by dedicated wine enthusiasts. The key word is "usually."

Because this may vary, there is one surefire way to find out. Just ask the question, "Have you personally tasted this wine?" Any employee who has not tasted the wine but can talk about how smooth and supple the tannins are is just spouting back at you the PR marketing wine-speak created and provided by the wine wholesaler. Find a place where the staff knows what it is selling. It will generally be a couple of bucks more expensive than the mega discount bottle store, but you will save money in the long run—and maybe make a trusted wine friend as well.

Some wine retailers have gone to the trouble and expense of procuring a license to allow tasting in their establishment. A place like this understands your need to taste something before purchasing. A fee may be charged for the privilege, but it should be well worth the expense to you if you can purchase your bottle knowing what it tastes like to you, not to someone else. We all have our own palates, and what the employee likes does not translate to what you like all the time.

It is also for this reason that I suggest you visit your local winery and do a tasting **flight.** A flight is simply a series of wines, no more than five (remember palate fatigue) and usually about three, with a common link among them. It may simply be that they are all from the same winery, as you may find in a tasting room, but a flight you have elsewhere could be three different producers' zinfandel (or other varietal)—zinfandels from the same producer but from different vintages, or zinfandels from different appellations.

Every state in the country has a bonded commercial winery that makes wine they want you to try. Granted, some of these wineries make wine from fruit other than grapes, but you owe it to yourself to check out what is local and available, and it may just be delicious. I have tasted wine made from pineapple in Hawaii, blueberries in Maine, and strawberries in Germany, all of which were fermented dry and which you would have difficulty identifying as a fruit wine if they were served to you **blind,** concealed in a bag. They may not have been cutting edge in the wine blogs, and I assure you no national reviewer is going to give them notice any more than they are about to review a tiny producer stuck up in the hills somewhere, but they tasted darned good. Unless you take the initiative, you will never discover just how good an obscure fruit wine or cabernet or zinfandel or syrah from some winery you have never heard of can be.

24

How to act in a tasting room

24

How to act in a tasting room

I have personally operated the tasting bar at my winery for the past eight years, and let me tell you, friends, what I have experienced there is what prompted a section on tasting room behavior in this book.

The disgusting but humorous scene in the movie *Sideways* where the character drinks the dump bucket seems to have triggered a sense that tasting rooms are for hilarity. You can certainly have fun in a tasting room, but the place should be approached more as a source of information than a source of amusement and hilarity. The film was just plain fiction, and similar behavior on your part is likely to land you in trouble with the sheriff. I'll explain more about the sheriff's role later.

When you walk into a typical winery tasting room, you will likely find a stand-up bar arrangement with a knowledgeable person ready to serve you, and an assortment of bottles all surrounded by other retail goods. This may be a tasting room to you, but it is the winery's retail store. You will generally not see any barstools, as this is not a bar in the sense you are going to buy a drink and hang out all afternoon or evening.

If you handle it right, this could be an excellent opportunity for you to add files to your tasting database folder. If you handle it poorly, all you are going to get are some tastes of wine. It's not like you need to approach the "expert" as if he were some high priest of wine, but even the smallest winery is going to staff its tasting bar with people who know more about their wines than you do. So in alignment with our strategy to suck information about these wines from the "expert," here's what *not* to do:

1. Act as if you know all there is to know about wine.
2. Order the server about or be less-than-totally polite ("Gimme some of that cabernet").
3. Make less-than-friendly comments about the wine or take a sip and dump the rest in the bucket without comment. If you hate the wine, ask the server to pour you less because you are driving.
4. Confront about personal wine points and preferences ("This zinfandel is too tannic").

Do have some idea of what kinds of wines you enjoy. If you tell the pourer, "I don't know, you pick them for me," without any guidance at all, you are telling that person you don't know anything about the subject and really don't care. Believe it or not, when I ask people, "Red or white?" some do not voice a preference. That doesn't exactly set up an educational dialogue, does it?

You need to put some energy into the situation or you will get next to nothing out of it. When offered a taste of something, hula-hoop your glass according to the instructions in this book. That alone will catch the attention of the pourer, who is used to seeing 90 percent of the people on your side of the bar take a passing sniff as they gulp down their sample.

When your nose comes out of that glass, your eyes should be closed (the better to focus), and you must say something descriptive. Just don't let it be something like "cat piss," which is a legitimate descriptor of some sauvignon blanc. Although "cat piss," which you may have read about in a magazine, will get a guffaw from others at the bar and make you the center of attention for a millisecond, the pourer, who makes a living selling wine, is going to be pissed in a totally different way because two other tasters rolled their eyes and left as the third poured his wine into the dump bucket in response to your silliness.

Although "cat piss," "barnyard," and "manure" are all legitimate descriptors of wine components, they are alarming to people who do not understand the nuances with or the context in which they should be used. Your attempt at humor does nothing in terms of developing a rapport and some understanding of the winery's wines.

If, on the other hand, when your nose comes out of the glass, you say some generally positive thing, such as, "Nice fruit!" you can build on that comment with further comments and questions.

If the tasting bar is crowded, as is often the case at events, accept your taste and move away from the bar to allow others access. It's only polite. And you want to leave that pourer thinking you are the most interested and attentive person in the place, just as the pourer wants you to think the tasting room is the friendliest and informative wine place. Being polite and interested is the way you get a special pour of the ten-year-old reserve that was opened at a party earlier that day.

The close interaction with the pourer is a powerful way to learn about the wines, wine terms, and perhaps even winemaking. If you cannot get access to the pourer, who may be pouring wine for eight or ten people, interact with the person on your left or right. If you do this in a comfortable way, it is a great way to learn from someone and perhaps make a wine friend. A winery tasting room is a friendly place with few of the outwardly obvious aspects of a lounge or Joe's Bar and Grill.

Women, particularly, seem more comfortable coming into a tasting room alone than they do going into a bar. Maybe that's because most tasting rooms are far more civilized than Joe's Bar and Grill. I guess

I am surprised more single guys haven't figured that out yet.

When you are finished with your wine-tasting education, thank and maybe tip the pourer (there's probably a jar) and buy a bottle of wine to take with you. Ultimately, you are voting for or against a winery with your wallet or pocketbook every time you make a wine purchase.

Oh, yes, the sheriff. We have a tendency to think of winery tasting rooms as different from Joe's Bar, in part because of the environs. Five tastes of wine might be just over a glass in total, but if you have been to a different winery tasting earlier, have not eaten much before the tasting, weigh less than 130 pounds and know you are a "lightweight" who gets tipsy or buzzed easily, be very, very careful. You could be blowing in the wrong zone of the breathalyzer scale if you get pulled over. Best of all, have a designated driver, reward that person with something nice (dinner certificate for two at a great local restaurant), and it will be worth the expense if you can taste without worry and way less than the cost of a DUI if you are caught driving.

25

Case for buying a
case of wine

25

Case for buying a case of wine

Instead of buying bottles of wine one at a time when you think about it, there are lots of good reasons to spring for a whole case. That's usually twelve bottles, for the uninitiated. Before you go all superior haughty on me, let me add that certain bottles are packaged eighteen to the case—too heavy to carry—and others six bottles to the case, popular packaging in Italian wines.

First of all, you *will* use more wine if you have

a case squirreled away in your "cellar," a cool dark place where you can successfully store your hoard. Let's make the assumption that you have purchased a case of a wine you like a lot. Don't you think you will:

- Be more inclined to open a bottle of the wine you know is tasty when your friend comes over for a visit?
- Be more inclined to bring a bottle to your mother's for the barbecue she and your dad are throwing this weekend?
- Be faster at pulling a cork when you and your spouse or partner have the unexpected opportunity to have an informal dinner alone because the kids are all at friends' houses for sleepovers?
- Be more confident giving a bottle as a gift than buying and giving a bottle of wine you have not tasted?
- Become part of the expanding group of people who look to wine as part of their normal life, rather than having it solely for something special? (I read a statistic that said more wine is consumed in the U.S. from Thanksgiving

Day to January 1 than all the rest of the year combined. I find that sad, and not because I earn part of my living in the wine industry.)

Another benefit of buying a case is that you will have the educational opportunity to taste the same wine bottled from the same batch over the course of several months or years. You can experience the subtle changes and nuances of aging, as long as you pay attention.

Finally, and the true motivating factor for many case purchases, is that you generally receive a discount of between 10 to 15 percent off the full retail price when you buy an entire case at once. Some wine discount stores and supermarkets will not offer case discounts, so ask before you assume anything.

I think I make a good case for buying a case.

26

Leftover wine

26

Leftover wine

I am assuming your house is wine normal and you have had this experience: after opening many bottles of wine for a party or dinner for several friends, at evening's end, you have a collection of bottles, some completely empty and some still containing wine. I have several helpful hints for you.

First, take note of which bottles have no wine left in them. Among winemakers, that is the test of a wine that will sell well. Forget your numbers, reviews, and ratings—the bottles that are empty at the end of the event are the ones people like to drink. Conversely, those with wine left in them are less favored, regardless of price or pedigree.

The next thought is what to do with all those small amounts of leftover wine. Here's what I do, assuming I have had all I want to drink: I pour all of them into one bottle, making my own secret blend. The purpose here is to fill a bottle up to the top so I can place a stopper or cork into it and keep the air out overnight. Sometimes this takes a combination of different sized bottles, but it keeps the wine blend (usually mostly red) drinkable until my next step, usually a day or longer later.

After at least a day, I make wine coolers out of the leftovers. Fill to the top of the glass the following: ice, red wine blend, and lemon or lime soda (such as Sprite or 7UP). For a more adult taste, try quinine water or tonic. If you are curling your lip at this moment, it is only because you have never tasted a wine cooler. Under a different brand name and with a slightly different formulation, these wine coolers were a mainstay of my young adult life. I only wish I'd had the idea to bottle them as a branded product.

Yet another variation is to use the leftover blend

to make sangria, which, as my friend Martin asserts, is Spanish for "headache." If you drink it out in the sun, I'll agree you could get a hammering head, but sipped in moderation at the restful end of a hard day, sangria can be a refreshing new taste. There are as many different recipes for sangria as there are for potato salad, but I like this one:

1. Dice a whole orange, lemon, and apple.
2. Place, juice and all, in a large pitcher.
3. Add up to a quarter cup of granulated white sugar and two to three bottles of red wine blend and a quarter bottle of brandy.
4. Stir until sugar is dissolved; refrigerate until cold.

This is a pure case of waste not, want not. Just because wine is left over doesn't mean it should be left out.

But what if you don't have six partial bottles left over? What if it is just you and your sweetie who decided not to finish the bottle of very special viognier and you want to save it for your next wine encounter? The answer is gas. Argon gas is much heavier than air and forms a blanket of gas over the wine, keeping the air away and eliminating oxidation. We use this in the winery to protect partially filled containers. We purchase it by the tank, but it also comes in a can for about ten bucks and lasts for 120 uses. If you throw wine away because it goes bad on you, buy some. The product I have been using and recommending for years is called Private Preserve (www.privatepreserve.com). Complete instructions for use are printed on the can.

27

Wine clubs: wine from the source

27

Wine clubs: wine from the source

At one point during your winery tasting room visit, you will notice literature about or listen to a pitch about the winery's wine club. Should you consider it? What should you look for? What's normal?

A good club treats you right with benefits that include free tastings, first shots at limited editions, special wines not in distribution, discounts on wine you purchase (20 percent is about normal), and perhaps invitations to special events at a reduced cost. You should also expect a dialogue with the winemakers so you can continue to further your wine education.

In return, you agree to buy a certain number of bottles at a certain frequency. Two bottles every other month is entirely reasonable. The cost will be charged to your credit account. You should receive a club discount on these selections, and they should be shipped to you, or if the club is flexible, you can arrange to pick them up at the tasting room.

Most clubs I have experienced are less than flexible. The larger they are, the less flexible they become. This is because it is much easier to administer to a 200-member club than a 2,000-member club. Any change in the normal process (Mr. Jones wants only white wine) makes the administration process more difficult.

It's easy to get caught up in the enthusiasm of the moment. When you join, you should have a good idea what this club is going to cost at whatever interval it is going to process your order. Keep an eye on your credit card statement as shipping and billing mistakes do happen.

If you see that you are receiving only the most

expensive wines on the winery's list, you may want to reevaluate the cost-benefit of the club to you. On the other hand, if you see you are paying top dollar for very ordinary wines in your shipments, who needs the club? You can buy ordinary low-end wines at any supermarket for less than any winery will sell them to you.

This brings me to why clubs are valuable to wineries. When you step into the tasting room, taste some wines and learn from the pourer, then decide to buy a bottle. The retail price you pay at the register is as high a retail price you would pay anywhere for that wine. This is not a bad thing for you because you have had the opportunity to taste the wine before buying, you know the wine has been handled and stored correctly, and you have (if you were astute) picked up some knowledge. If you purchased the same wine at the supermarket for $3 less, it's doubtful you would have any of those opportunities. Wineries discount their wines to wholesalers from 30 to 60 percent off retail prices, depending on the price point of the wine and the number of cases being sold. This means the wholesaler can have a lot of flexibility in selling the wine to the retailer who sells to you at the store.

It takes few math skills to realize that a bottle that retails at the winery for $20 is sold to a distributor or wholesaler at $10 then resold to a retailer for $13 can end up on the retailer's shelf for $17. This three-tier system has benefits for the huge winery corporations and is also the reason small wineries prefer not to be "in distribution." That three-tier system is also the reason you need to sign for your wine shipment at the door, and why the winery has such a fondness for its club membership. Think of it: if you had the opportunity to sell product at 20 percent discount to a consistent market—the club members—month after month, or to a distributor at 50 percent discount, which would you prefer? If you also consider the good club referrals to the winery's wines (inexpensive advertising), it's a no-brainer, whether the winery is in distribution or not.

You may be asking yourself, What was that he wrote up there? "That three-tier system is also the reason you need to sign for your wine shipment at the door?" Well, you can imagine if you were a wine distributor, letting a small winery on a hillside in California ship a case of wine directly to a wine aficionado in Michigan, how that might be viewed as a business threat, even if the distributor didn't carry the small winery's wines, which is usually the case. Big distributors don't have any interest in distributing small wineries' wines, no matter how good or unique. It's a money thing.

On May 16, 2005, the U.S. Supreme Court ruled that if a state allowed shipment of its own wineries' wines within the state, it could not prohibit the shipment of wine into the state from outside the state. This ruling is still being interpreted in the courts five years later, but one by one, states are allowing direct shipment, usually under some conditions. In the middle of all this, the incredible issue was raised that minors would be able to buy wine and have it shipped to them at home. Okay, I admit, it's possible. I don't think teenagers are drinking $200 cases of cabernet sauvignon, but that's me.

UPS is now required to have the recipient or some other adult who must be sober (I am not making this up) sign for a wine shipment. If you are one of those people who work all day and you can have the wine shipped to your office, use that address. If you have a neighbor who is home most of the time, ask to use that address. Barring all other choices, ask a local merchant where you are a known customer if you could have the wine shipped to that address and signed for. Then catch your UPS or FedEx driver and explain the situation.

Wine clubs have advantages and generally are worthwhile to become part of, particularly if there is the opportunity for a personal connection to the winery.

28

Wine is in the moment

28

Wine is in the moment

As a winemaker I spend more time than most people sniffing and peering at wine, holding it to the light, and making notes. Eventually I take some in my mouth and roll it around over my tongue with great slurping noises as I mix it with air to test every edge of the wine for the flavors I may find there. Then I spend even more time talking about what I have discovered with other wine tasters, some experienced, some not.

Since I started making wine in 1974, I have realized that this clinical approach to wine tasting can deliver a detailed analysis of different wines, complete with numerical scales against which they can be compared, but it bears almost no relationship to how real people experience a glass of wine.

When you experience a wine, you incorporate so much more than the wine itself into your appreciation that the analytical part is overshadowed and becomes much less important than the subjective part.

Can you remember sitting, glass in hand, under the arbor one night, candle's glow bouncing off your companion's face outlined against the night, talking about whatever of life's intimacies you bumped into as your conversation drifted like a lazy raft down a slow river? Or perhaps you sat on your broad front porch, or beside a dying campfire at the beach, or at a wonderful restaurant talking and drinking wine, savoring the moment without even being totally conscious of doing it.

Those wines, the ones I shared with special people, are the ones I remember with far greater fondness and clarity than any I have rated professionally with numbered samples lined up on a white table, notebook and pencil at hand.

So the next time you hear someone say, "The most incredible bottle of wine I have ever had," it will invariably be followed by a description of an intimate shared event. Drinking wine, like kissing, is most memorable when done with someone else.

29
Tasting blind

29

Tasting blind

I have said several times that the difference between tasting wine and drinking wine (both admirable pastimes) is the attention focus you bring to tasting. Let me introduce you to a focus tool you can easily use the next time you have a tasting party, or when you simply want you and a friend to test your wine senses to their limits.

Tasting "blind" is done by tasters having no information provided other than the identical numbered glasses that contain wine. The simplest way to do this is to recruit a third person to open the bottles in another room, pour the wine, and bring the glasses to the participants.

Often you see a competitive variation of this, which can work when a group of people are testing their tasting skills. This is done by lining up a number of bottles in paper bags with their corks removed (from the room), and writing numbers on the bags. This is fun but might not be as blind as you think. Here are some clues you can garner from the bottle-in-the-bag variation:

- The shape of the bottle (bordeaux varietals are in one shape, burgundy varietals are in another);
- The color of the foil—if showing, it can be distinctive and reveal the producer of the wine;
- The thickness of the bottle lip, which can show if it is a domestic or imported wine.

Like a poker player looking for a "tell," any of these clues can give a taster an educated guess and an advantage in determining the wine's origin or qualities.

Why go through all this work? Tasting wines blind is important because the moment your eye falls upon a label, your impression is skewed either in favor or against the wine. I have two examples from my own experience to share with you.

When I was very early into my wine education, maybe twenty-two, learning at an enormous rate, a foursome of my friends and I were at a picnic in a park. We had shared some wines, if you get my drift. One member of the group pulled a bottle from his backpack almost filled with wine into which the cork had been pushed. It had a very fancy French label (this was before I knew much about French labels). He offered it up as a wine he had had the night before at a dinner party. He poured me a sample and asked what I thought. I told him I thought it was good, at which he howled with laughter as he told me he had filled the bottle at home with the most common of jug wines just so he would have it in a container he could bring on the picnic. I had been fooled by my glimpse of the label into thinking that there was quality where there was not. There is a huge lesson there.

Another time, much later in my wine education, I was at an informal backyard dinner party after bottling wine. One of my wine friends brought me a bottle in a paper bag, handed it to me and said it was a viognier and asked me what I thought of it. At this point in my life, I was much less naive when handed a wine sample. I paid attention to the wine and after some consideration of its nice acid balance, peachy fruit and hint of sweetness, pronounced it "excellent, give me a whole glass." My friend howled with laughter and tore the paper from the bottle to reveal that it was indeed a viognier from North Carolina! There is no way I would have been as receptive to the quality of that wine if I had been shown the label before the tasting. Is that because I am a provincial wine snob? No, it's because I am human and have my own personal beliefs, prejudices and opinions, just like you. (If you are from the North Carolina wine industry you are probably gnashing your teeth right now, but take heart. I have done you a lot of good with this story over the years!)

Once you have built some confidence in your wine-tasting skills, arrange to have someone open and pour in a different room and present to you blind three of your favorite wines, wines you really think you know and have had experience drinking and tasting. If you can honestly and correctly identify all three of those wines, you should be proud, because it is very difficult for most people to accomplish. It's important to use three because if you miss one, you have missed two. If there are only two wines, you have a 50-50 chance of being correct.

Try it. Testing your blind tasting skills can be educational and fun.

30
Spitting in public

30

Spitting in public

If you are caught spitting in public in Singapore, you will be fined hundreds of U.S. dollars. I wonder if that law applies to wine-tasting events open to the public. It could be a good revenue generator.

It is important for you to know about this practice so that the first time you witness it, you are not so surprised that you drop your wineglass.

The practice of "spitting" wine started long ago with professionals who may have been required to "taste" upwards of twenty wines at a morning sitting. Rather than become inebriated, which brings a delightful comedic scene to mind, professional tasters would sample the wine, test its attributes by all the means discussed elsewhere in this book, and then expectorate the wine rather than swallow it. They claimed this gave them all the information they needed to evaluate the wine, including an evaluation of the finish.

This practice has morphed from the professional necessity to the affected amateur attempting to impress someone with his knowledge (it's almost always guys who spit in public). In practical terms there is almost no occasion I can think of in which you may need to spit. But in the event you need to keep alcohol out of your bloodstream, if you're taking medication, if you're driving and paranoid, or if you're just trying to stay completely sober, let's review the proper procedure.

First, locate the spitting receptacle. After you have taken the wine into your mouth and done your tasting of its components, pick up the receptacle and bring it to your mouth and gently expectorate. If the receptacle is too large and heavy, you are allowed to bend your head to the receptacle and gently expectorate into it. The objective is to get rid of the wine with as little noise as possible. Don't be surprised if you get a reaction from your fellow tasters, something like "Eew!" or "Yuck!" You may be comfortable offering the explanation, "I'm going to a big wine tasting and want to save my sobriety."

Now you know.

31

Knowledge and creativity: building your database files

31

Knowledge and creativity: building your database files

The other day I was watching a taped cooking show on TV, something I do for relaxation, and the chef from the CIA (Culinary Institute of America, not the Central Intelligence Agency) was assembling a fish dish containing fennel and other aromatic vegetables. As he finished, he said, "Now if I were serving a wine with this, it would be?"

"Sauvignon blanc," said he and I at the same moment.

This seemed somehow more pleasing than knowing the answer to a question on *Jeopardy*, and I wondered why that particular wine had popped into my head. Why not chardonnay, or Riesling, or chenin blanc, or even Gewurztraminer, all white wines?

The reason is that I have tasted all those white wines and many reds and therefore had the knowledge that sauvignon blanc would complement the flavors in the dish. I had literally tasted the dish in my mental palate and selected sauvignon blanc from my wine-tasting database as the wine on target. Now before you start thinking this winemaker has been spending too many hours tasting barrel samples in the cellar, let me tell you that in the future, you could easily do the same matchup.

If you taste wines carefully and really pay attention to what is happening in your mouth and the data coming to you through smell and sight, you will know those wines generally by taste and know how they are different from each other.

But Paul, you say, there are hundreds of chardonnays, maybe thousands. True, and some are terrible, some are elegant, some are buttery, and some are acidic, but all come from the same grape and have some common varietal characteristics of flavor that you should be able to use to classify and say in your mind's palate, "*This* is what chardonnay tastes like." The same with Riesling and Gewurztraminer, which stands out like a red chili pepper. Maybe you should start with that one and see what I mean about a wine's varietal characteristics.

As you know, most people drink wine and not very many taste it. Yes, they may give the glass a sniff and pause after their first gulp to say, "Oh, nice!" but very few literally savor the subtle nuances of wine, particularly white. They are busy eating and talking. And that's cool, because that's why we make it.

But if you pay attention, you will be building your knowledge about specific wines. Your brain files this information away as a database in that computer you carry between your ears, retrieving that knowledge at will. With this knowledge, you can recall dishes to complement your wines, or recall wines to complement your dishes.

32

Murder by heat

32

Murder by heat

It is not lost to me that I carry a concern for my wines throughout their "lives." When someone purchases a case of wine at my winery and I place it in the trunk of their automobile, the lecture is automatically cued: "Don't leave this in here too long, and if you have to stop on the way home, park in the shade."

But then I am the kind of person who if going shopping for wine on a warm day, brings along an ice chest with a top that closes tightly and a few ice cubes in a plastic bag to keep the contents from heating up.

I have read that it can get up to 140 degrees Fahrenheit in the trunk of a car parked in the sun on a warm day, and we both know that a hot car can melt the heck out of a Hershey bar! Wine literally cooks in that level of heat and if tasted later, has a dead, red liquid, but not a wine flavor.

I once visited a friend's new home, and he mentioned that he thought some of the wine he had purchased from me was going bad. After I removed the knife from my heart, we took a look and saw what he considered a fine, out-of-the-way storage place for the wine—on top of his refrigerator! Given the heat and vibration that is inherent in the refrigeration process, I was amazed that any of my creations had survived there.

In another instance of death by heat, one winter I was at a small restaurant in Louisiana when upon studying their wine list, I discovered a very nice California cabernet sauvignon from a decade-old vintage at a price I could not believe. With all the anticipation of someone who had discovered a Rembrandt at a garage sale, I asked the waiter if I could see the bottle (which I hope you appreciate is different from ordering a bottle). To my dismay, he retrieved one from the wine rack which was located over the radiator.

For your knowledge base, here's what a bottle looks like that has been overheated and killed. If the bottle has been stored properly on its side, the cork will probably have pushed out and made a bulge in the foil capsule (usually tin or plastic) that covers the cork. When you remove the foil, you will find evidence of wine that has pushed past the cork as the wine heated up and expanded. Once the cork seal has been compromised, the avenue of bacterial infection has opened up, and spoilage could have begun. However, if the wine got really hot, bacterial spoilage is not the main issue. One hundred–plus degrees of heat deadens all the flavors of the wine and causes a metamorphosis of the liquid to something else. Try this at home by taking a cup of a favorite red wine, putting it in a nonreactive (stainless steel) pan, and heating it up to a near-simmer. Let it cool down and taste it compared to a glass of the same wine that has not been heated. Yuck.

Heat is the enemy of fine wine. Keep it cool and alive.

33

Restaurant behaviors

33

Restaurant behaviors

Your newly acquired wine knowledge and experience will not go unnoticed by friends and family who are mistakenly under the impression that wine is a complicated and intimidating subject. In fact, even by the time you are halfway through this book, you may be considered the "wine expert," at least relative to your friends' and family's level of knowledge.

So here's what happens: you all go to a restaurant,

and whoever is paying for the outing, even if you are sharing that responsibility, hands the wine list to you and says, "You pick the wine." My first reaction would be to ask what the budget is, but that is not always the polite thing to do. The only time you would order the wine before choosing the food is when you are with a group of wine aficionados who want to try a specific wine and match their food choices to it, so the prudent thing to do is find out what people are ordering so as to complement those choices. However, this knowledge can also cause confusion over the choice of wine if people are ordering diverse dishes (e.g., from steak to fish).

This is when your wine knowledge and experience will shine. You will know that lighter reds, pinot noir and Italian varietals, depending on how they were made, will go with both ends of the spectrum. One reason pinot noir is so popular is because of this diverse ability. However, you also know that pinot noir and any red wine can be made into a dark tannic monster, so if you are not familiar with one of the light reds on the list, you fall back on your second line of defense: the wine waiter, wine steward, or sommelier, his title depending on the price point of the restaurant. This person is your friend, so you should get to know him. He will have tasted and will know about all the wines on the wine list. You might say something like, "We are having different dishes and I thought a pinot noir or a lighter Italian varietal would be good to go with them all. Which would you recommend?" Unless you are at dinner with Bill Gates, expect that the wine choices suggested will be in the mid-range and perhaps a little higher. There is no shame in asking for help from the resident wine authority; the price of this service is included in the wine markup, which you will notice is quite considerable.

Another strategy to employ when your dinner companions are ordering diverse courses is to order a dry white wine and a heavier red wine. The thought is that everyone will have a small glass of white to start and red later if appropriate to their main courses.

So, perhaps with the help of staff, you have chosen a wine or wines. Your job is done, you think, and you can sit back and relax. Out come the wines, and the waiter presents the bottle for your approval. Once receiving your approval in the form of a nod (you having checked that it was the correct wine and vintage for which someone is paying so dearly), the server proceeds to pull the cork. Once done, he presents you with the cork and pours a small taste into your glass. Here's what you are supposed to do, and why.

With the cork, do nothing unless you notice that the server has not smelled it, in which case you should, checking for the TCA, which tells you this is the extremely rare bottle that is "corked" (see Chapter 13, Corked wine and TCA). If, as should have happened, you notice that the server has indeed sniffed the cork, leave it alone.

You should now examine, swirl, and sniff the wine in your glass, which should tell you all you need to know. If it is oxidized and murky, as if it had been stored over a radiator in Louisiana, ask for the server's opinion. If it is terrible, you can refuse it, but the server will have withdrawn it before you have the opportunity. No restaurant worth its toque is going to serve bad wine or argue with you. However, this should be done without the drama and emotion you have seen in similar scenes on television or in the movies. And, I might add, in my decades of eating and ordering wine in restaurants with wine lists, I have never had to send a wine back because it was not palatable. I did not need to send the Louisiana wine back because I never actually ordered it, due to the bulge in its foil.

Other restaurant issues lurk. If the white wine is presented along with an ice bucket but is already chilled, the server should leave the ice bucket, but you should ask that the remaining wine be left in the bottle on the table. Wine served too cold is tasteless, so realistically, an ice bucket (also called a champagne bucket) is needed only if the wine is at room temperature and needs to be chilled. A third of a bottle will become way too cold to taste in just a minute or two. Sparkling wines are, of course, served much colder than still whites, so the ice bucket is appropriate for them.

Here's another move: if you are ordering a red wine and the bottle presented feels warm to your touch, you are authorized to ask the wine server to place it in the ice bucket for a couple of minutes to help it cool off. You are looking to achieve 68 degrees Fahrenheit, a temperature possibly cooler than the ambient temperature of the restaurant in July. If the wine is coming to you from temperature-controlled storage, all is well, but if not, you deserve to have it served at the optimum temperature because you are paying a premium price for this bottle. Again, no restaurant worth its reputation is going to refuse or even hesitate to accommodate you.

In doing this, are you being a wine snob? Think back to how we defined that person early in the book. If you are using knowledge in a non-objectionable way to improve your wine experience or that of your friends, you are no wine snob. How you talk to the wine server and make your requests is as important in defining yourself as what you are saying to him.

34

Store your treasures, but use them

34

Store your treasures, but use them

Okay. We are almost finished. You have paid attention and learned a lot about what wine is and how you can enjoy it in all its mysterious complexity. Now, the wine world is at your feet, with literally *millions* of different bottles beckoning your corkscrew. Hey, there are over 50,000 producers in Italy alone, so your work is cut out for you.

Something I failed to mention is that most European wines are called by the names of where they originate, not by the name of the varietal as they are in the United States. So you will find that Chianti is mostly Sangiovese, Burgundy is pinot noir, German Rhine wine is Riesling. These are facts you can sit down and memorize (though it's a very long list) or learn by experiencing. It's probably best that you start by experimenting and experiencing with American varietals and then branch out internationally.

As you start to make personal discoveries, you are going to want to acquire some wines to save, which is different from cellaring. You save wines for anticipated special events, or for the not-so-distant unknown future; you cellar wines long-term to see how they mature.

If you start to acquire some special bottles, you are going to need to store them safely (see Chapter 32, Murder by heat). No, you don't need to spend $800 on a temperature-controlled storage unit (but which are really nice, by the way). Depending on where you live in the United States, storing your bottles in a narrow range of temperature (60 to 70 degrees Fahrenheit) will be an easy-to-difficult task. Interestingly, San Francisco has a very even cool temperature for all the California wine stored there, but on rare days, the temperature spikes in the 90s and even to 100. That makes it way too hot to leave your collection to fend for itself in the dining room rack, even though that place was perfect the rest of the year.

It's a lot hotter where I lived just fifteen minutes north of San Francisco, but I use the same storage method I would recommend for a San Franciscan. I purchased a large ice chest with a tight lid, in which my special bottles could fit easily. I have only eighteen to twenty bottles at a time because I use my wines for the purpose for which they were intended, not so they will appreciate or become collectors' items. I place the chest on the floor of a closet, physically in the center of my home, where walls are not directly exposed to the sun. I make sure that I have room in the chest for a small blue artificial ice block, one of the blue ones you can refreeze. I pop it into the chest along with an inexpensive min-max thermometer and close the lid. I have discovered that if the wines were cooled before going into the chest, this method works very well for short-term heat or cold spikes.

If you have an unheated basement that is at least six feet under the ground surface, the space is a perfect place to start that same min-max thermometer to see the temperature range over time. Just remember that the air temperature is different from the liquid temperature of a wine bottle. To judge the wine temperature more accurately, put your min-max thermometer in a quart jar of water, which will change temperature more slowly.

Where there is a need, you can find a way. Remember you are shooting for a minimal range of fluctuation in temperature, not a minimum temperature. I have even used twelve-hole Styrofoam shippers, inserted my cooled wine, and duct-taped the seams closed. Not only does that stabilize the temperature, but the bother of unsealing makes one hesitate unless one is really serious about getting to a bottle.

It's not hard to get carried away with collecting wine for personal use. It starts innocently enough—a few prime bottles on sale at a local wine shop, a case here and a case there, "finds" of wine you have tasted and know are good and will probably get better. If, as a friend of mine did, you find yourself taking bids with contractors to dig a wine cellar into the rock behind your house and you are seriously considering a $30,000 bid to do so, you may want to seriously reassess your wine-storage goals and needs.

It's difficult to imagine going that far, but I often hear from people who complain that they have a nice wine collection and no one with whom to drink it. This is because they (and you) don't want to share your coddled cabernet with someone who would just as soon be drinking supermarket zinfandel. If you wait too long, your wines will go over the top and start to degrade, which is a crying shame.

So don't let it go that far. Drinking wine is a social event; I almost never open a bottle of wine just for myself. And you should also appreciate the opportunity you have in your collection to open the senses and mouths of all kinds of friends. Host tasting parties where your guests taste wines blind, and see if your expensive cabernet rates any higher than the other entries. This is not a competition—it's an experience and lots of fun.

Personally, I encourage you all to try those potentially wonderful wines and even the ones that are less so, as you open up your mind to new wines from new places. Go for it.

Wine word lookup and quiz

Wine word lookup and quiz

CPSIA information can be obtained at www.ICGtesting.com
Printed in the USA
LVOW12s1408160714

394625LV00001B/45/P